# EDMONDS

## *Illustrated*

# COOKBOOK II

# EDMONDS

## Illustrated

# COOKBOOK II

**EDMONDS**

# CONTENTS

INTRODUCTION 7

## BAKING 9
Cakes 10

Biscuits 24

Slices 30

Muffins, Loaves and Tartlets 40

## FINGER FOODS 47

## LIGHT MEALS AND SALADS 61
Light Meals 62

Salads 78

## MAIN MEALS 89

## DESSERTS 121

## FESTIVE AND TRADITIONAL FARE 139
Christmas 140

Easter 148

Traditional Fare 150

Barbecue Menu 162

## PRESERVES 165

## ICINGS, PASTRIES, DRESSINGS AND SAUCES 178

WEIGHTS AND MEASURES 184

GLOSSARY 186

INDEX 190

ACKNOWLEDGEMENTS 192

# INTRODUCTION

Over ninety years ago Edmonds published the first edition of a modest cookery book of economical, everyday recipes that quickly captured the culinary imagination of New Zealanders and soon secured a place in virtually every Kiwi household. Following the phenomenal success of the *Edmonds Illustrated Cookbook* in 1998, the *Edmonds Illustrated Cookbook II* presents more of the Edmonds heritage, while reflecting the changing tastes of New Zealanders in a fast-moving, global world.

Featuring over 220 carefully tested recipes, this wonderfully illustrated book places the same emphasis as the original *Edmonds Cookery Book* on ease of preparation, economy and great tasting dishes the whole household can enjoy.

Continuing in the Edmonds baking tradition, the opening section features chapters on Cakes, Biscuits, Slices and Muffins, Loaves and Tartlets. The sections that follow on Finger Foods, Light Meals and Salads, Main Meals and Desserts offer a range of traditional and exciting new culinary delights to tempt all members of the household. Festive and Traditional Fare presents fresh approaches to old-time favourites to ensure success on those special memorable occasions, while the section on Preserves includes tempting conserves and spreads. Icings, Pastries, Dressings and Sauces will prove an invaluable section for handy reference.

It is heartening to realise the providing and sharing of food has not lost its importance in the daily lives of New Zealanders. Edmonds recognises both the value of tradition and the desire for fresh approaches to food. The *Edmonds Illustrated Cookbook II* brings both together with this superb selection of recipes. We hope you enjoy cooking from this book.

*The Edmonds Team, July 2000*

# BAKING

# CAKES

# ALMOND CRUMBLE CAKE

125 g butter, softened
¾ cup caster sugar
2 eggs
¼ teaspoon almond essence
1½ cups Champion standard
   grade flour
2 teaspoons Edmonds baking powder
70 g packet ground almonds
1 cup milk

### CRUMBLE TOPPING
½ cup Champion standard grade flour
2 tablespoons brown sugar
70 g packet sliced almonds
¼ cup melted butter

Cream butter and sugar until light and fluffy. Add eggs one at a time, beating well after each addition. Beat in essence. Sift together flour and baking powder. Fold into creamed mixture alternately with ground almonds and milk. Spoon into a greased 20-cm-diameter cake tin that has the base lined with baking paper. Scatter crumble topping over cake. To make the topping, combine all ingredients in a bowl. Mix well. Bake at 180°C for 50–55 minutes or until a skewer inserted in the centre of the cake comes out clean. Leave cake in tin for 15 minutes before turning onto a wire rack to cool.

# APPLE SULTANA CAKE

1 cup sultanas
2 cups peeled, cored and diced apple
   (2 medium apples)
1¼ cups water
1 teaspoon Edmonds baking soda
125 g butter, softened

1 cup sugar
1 egg
1 teaspoon vanilla essence
2 cups Champion standard grade flour
1 teaspoon Edmonds baking powder
1 teaspoon cinnamon

Combine sultanas, apple and water in a saucepan. Bring to the boil over a low heat. Simmer for 3–4 minutes. Remove from heat. Stir in baking soda. Cool. Cream butter and sugar until light and fluffy. Add egg and beat well. Beat in essence. Sift together flour, baking powder and cinnamon. Fold apple mixture and dry ingredients alternately into creamed mixture. Transfer to a greased 22-cm-diameter cake tin that has had the base lined with baking paper. Bake at 180°C for 1 hour or until a skewer inserted in centre of cake comes out clean. Leave cake in tin for 10 minutes before turning onto a wire rack to cool. *(Opposite, middle right)*

# CHOCOLATE CHIP SPECKLE CAKE

175 g butter, softened
1½ cups sugar
4 eggs
1 teaspoon vanilla essence

1½ cups Champion standard
  grade flour
1½ teaspoons Edmonds baking powder
¾ cup chocolate chips

Cream butter and sugar until light and fluffy. Add eggs one at a time, beating well after each addition. Beat in essence. Sift together flour and baking powder. Fold into creamed mixture with chocolate chips. Spoon mixture into a well-greased 22-cm-diameter baba tin. Bake at 180°C for 55–60 minutes or until a skewer inserted in the centre of the cake comes out clean. Leave cake in tin for 10 minutes before turning onto a wire rack.

N.B. A 22-cm-diameter fancy ring mould tin can be used instead of a baba tin.

# CINNAMON PECAN CAKE

100 g pecan nuts
125 g butter, softened
1 cup caster sugar
2 eggs
1 teaspoon vanilla essence
1½ cups Champion standard
   grade flour
1½ teaspoons Edmonds baking powder
1 teaspoon cinnamon
¾ cup milk

COFFEE CREAM FILLING
75 g butter, softened
1 cup icing sugar
1 teaspoon instant coffee
icing sugar to dust

Place pecan nuts in a food processor. Pulse until ground. Cream butter and sugar until light and fluffy. Add eggs one at a time, beating well after each addition. Beat in essence. Fold in ground pecans. Sift together flour, baking powder and cinnamon. Fold into creamed mixture alternately with milk. Spoon into a greased 20-cm-diameter cake tin that has had the base lined with baking paper. Bake at 180°C for 45 minutes, or until a skewer inserted in the centre of the cake comes out clean. Leave cake in tin for 10 minutes before turning onto a wire rack. When cold, split cake in half horizontally. Place one half on a serving plate. Spread over Coffee Cream Filling then sandwich with remaining half of cake. To make the filling, beat together butter, icing sugar and coffee until smooth. Dust cake with icing sugar. If desired, cut star shapes out of baking paper and place on top of the cake before dusting with icing sugar.

# COCONUT CAKE

250 g butter, softened
1½ cups caster sugar
4 eggs
1 teaspoon vanilla essence
2 cups Champion standard grade flour

2 teaspoons Edmonds baking powder
1 cup coconut
White Icing (see page 179)
toasted thread coconut to garnish

Cream butter and sugar until light and fluffy. Add eggs one at a time, beating well after each addition. Beat in essence. Sift together flour and baking powder. Fold flour and coconut into creamed mixture. Spoon into a greased deep 24-cm-diameter ring tin that has had the base lined with baking paper. Bake at 180°C for 45 minutes or until a skewer inserted in the cake comes out clean. Leave cake in tin for 10 minutes before turning onto a wire rack. When cold, spread with White Icing and garnish with toasted coconut. *(Below left)*

# COFFEE CAKE

250 g butter, softened
1½ cups caster sugar
3 eggs
2 cups Champion standard grade flour
2 teaspoons Edmonds baking powder

2 tablespoons coffee and
 chicory essence
¾ cup milk
Coffee Icing (see page 179)

Cream butter and sugar until light and fluffy. Add eggs one at a time, beating well after each addition. Sift together flour and baking powder. Combine essence and milk. Fold dry ingredients and milk alternately into creamed mixture. Spoon into a deep 22-cm-diameter cake tin that has had the base lined with baking paper. Bake at 180°C for 50–55 minutes or until a skewer inserted in the centre of the cake comes out clean. Leave cake in tin for 10 minutes before turning onto a wire rack. When cold, spread with Coffee Icing. *(Above right)*

# DATE CAKE

125 g butter, softened
1/2 cup sugar
1 tablespoon lemon juice
1/4 teaspoon grated lemon zest
2 eggs

1 1/2 cups Champion standard grade flour
1 teaspoon Edmonds baking powder
1/4 cup milk
3/4 cup pitted, chopped dates
icing sugar to dust

Cream butter, sugar, lemon juice and zest until light and fluffy. In a separate bowl beat eggs until thick. Sift flour and baking powder together. Fold flour into creamed mixture alternately with eggs. Fold in milk and dates. Transfer to a greased 18-cm-diameter ring tin that has had the base lined with baking paper. Bake at 180°C for 30–40 minutes or until cake springs back when lightly touched. Leave in tin for 10 minutes before turning onto a wire rack. Just before serving, dust with icing sugar. *(Middle left)*

# GINGER ALE FRUIT CAKE

1 1/4 cups sultanas
1 1/4 cups pitted dates, halved
1 1/4 cups currants
1 1/4 cups raisins
1/4 cup mixed peel
300 ml ginger ale
225 g butter, softened

1 cup sugar
4 eggs
2 cups Champion standard grade flour
1 teaspoon Edmonds baking powder
1/4 teaspoon grated lemon zest
1/2 teaspoon vanilla essence
1/2 teaspoon almond essence

Combine sultanas, dates, currants, raisins and peel with the ginger ale in a large bowl. Cover and stand in a warm place overnight. The next day, cream butter and sugar until light and fluffy. Add eggs one at a time, beating well after each addition. Sift flour and baking powder together. Stir into creamed mixture. Add soaked fruit mixture, lemon zest, vanilla and almond essences. Stir well. Line a 20-cm square or 23-cm-diameter cake tin with two layers of brown paper followed by one layer of baking paper. Spoon mixture into tin. Bake at 140°C for 3 hours or until an inserted skewer comes out clean. Cool in tin. *(Top right)*

# GINGER CAKE

125 g butter, softened
1/2 cup sugar
3 tablespoons golden syrup
2 cups Champion standard grade flour
1 teaspoon Edmonds baking powder
1 teaspoon ground ginger
1 teaspoon mixed spice
2 eggs, beaten

1/4 cup chopped crystallised ginger
1/4 cup chopped walnuts
1/4 cup sultanas
1 teaspoon Edmonds baking soda
1 cup milk
White Icing (see page 179)
chopped crystallised ginger to garnish

Cream butter, sugar and golden syrup until light and fluffy. Sift flour, baking powder, ground ginger and mixed spice together. Add sifted dry ingredients to creamed mixture alternately with beaten eggs. Stir in chopped ginger, walnuts and sultanas. Dissolve baking soda in the milk and stir into mixture. Line a 20-cm square cake tin with baking paper. Pour mixture into tin. Bake at 180°C for 35 minutes. Leave in tin for 10 minutes before turning onto a wire rack. When cold, spread with White Icing. Garnish with crystallised ginger. *(Below)*

# LEMON CURD AND YOGHURT CAKE

250 g butter, softened
1½ cups caster sugar
4 eggs
finely grated zest of 1 lemon
2 cups Champion standard grade flour
2 teaspoons Edmonds baking powder

½ cup Lemon Curd (see page 179)
¾ cup natural unsweetened yoghurt
icing sugar to dust
citrus leaves to garnish
whipped cream to serve

Cream butter and sugar until light and fluffy. Add eggs one at a time, beating well after each addition. Beat in lemon zest. Sift flour and baking powder together. Combine lemon curd and yoghurt. Fold dry ingredients into creamed mixture alternately with lemon curd mixture. Spoon into a deep 22-cm-diameter cake tin that has been greased and lined with baking paper. Bake at 180°C for 50–55 minutes. Cool in tin. Dust with icing sugar and garnish with citrus leaves. Serve with cream.

# MOIST APPLE WALNUT CAKE

4 eggs
2 cups sugar
1 cup vegetable oil
1 cup roughly chopped walnuts
2 cups grated unpeeled Granny Smith
    apple (2 medium apples)
440 g can unsweetened crushed
    pineapple, drained

2 cups Champion standard grade flour
1½ teaspoons Edmonds baking powder
¾ teaspoon Edmonds baking soda
2 teaspoons cinnamon
1 teaspoon mixed spice
Cream Cheese Icing (see page 179)
chopped walnuts to garnish

Using a wooden spoon, beat together eggs, sugar and oil until sugar dissolves. Stir in walnuts, apple and pineapple. Combine flour, baking powder, soda and spices. Stir into egg mixture. Transfer to a greased deep 20-cm square cake tin that has had the base lined with baking paper. Bake at 180°C for 1¼ hours. Leave cake in tin for 15 minutes before transferring to a wire rack. When cold, spread with Cream Cheese Icing and garnish with chopped walnuts.

# MOIST CHOCOLATE CAKE

250 g butter, softened
1½ cups caster sugar
4 eggs
1 teaspoon vanilla essence
100 g dark chocolate melts, melted
1½ cups Champion standard
   grade flour

2 teaspoons Edmonds baking powder
½ cup cocoa
1 cup (250 g) sour cream
Melted Chocolate Icing (see page 179)

Cream butter and sugar until light and fluffy. Add eggs one at a time, beating well after each addition. Beat in essence and melted chocolate. Sift together flour, baking powder and cocoa. Fold sifted ingredients and sour cream alternately into creamed mixture. Transfer to a greased 24-cm-diameter cake tin that has had the base lined with baking paper. Bake at 180°C for 70 minutes, or until cake springs back when lightly pressed. Leave cake in tin for 10 minutes before turning onto a wire rack to cool. When cold, cut cake in half. Spread bottom half with Melted Chocolate Icing. Sandwich together with remaining half of cake.

# ORANGE POLENTA CAKE

125 g butter, softened
1 cup caster sugar
2 eggs
finely grated zest of 1 orange
¼ cup freshly squeezed orange juice
¼ cup orange marmalade

1 cup Champion standard grade flour
1 teaspoon Edmonds baking powder
½ cup polenta (cornmeal)
70 g packet ground almonds
½ cup milk
orange zest to garnish

Cream butter and sugar until light and fluffy. Add eggs one at a time, beating well after each addition. Beat in orange zest, juice and marmalade. Sift flour and baking powder together. Fold flour, polenta, almonds and milk into creamed mixture. Spoon into a 20-cm-diameter cake tin that has been greased and lined with baking paper. Bake at 180°C for 45 minutes or until a skewer inserted in the centre of the cake comes out clean. Leave cake in tin for 10 minutes before turning onto a wire rack. Garnish with orange zest.

# PLUM CAKE

200 g butter, softened
1 cup caster sugar
3 eggs
1 teaspoon vanilla essence
2 cups Champion standard grade flour
2 teaspoons Edmonds baking powder

70 g packet ground almonds
½ cup (125 g) sour cream
½ cup milk
6–8 firm, ripe plums, stoned
  and quartered
icing sugar to dust

Cream butter and sugar until light and fluffy. Add eggs one at a time, beating well after each addition. Beat in essence. Sift together flour and baking powder. Fold flour, almonds, sour cream and milk into creamed mixture. Spoon half of this batter over the bottom of a 22-cm-diameter cake tin that has had the base lined with baking paper. Arrange plums on top of the batter. Cover with remaining mixture. Bake at 160°C for 70 minutes or until cake springs back when pressed lightly. Leave cake in tin for 10 minutes before transferring to a cake rack. Just before serving, dust cake with icing sugar. *(Below left)*

# RHUBARB AND PECAN CRUST CAKE

### TOPPING
1 cup diced rhubarb
¾ cup toasted pecan nuts,
  roughly chopped
½ cup Champion standard grade flour
½ cup brown sugar
1 teaspoon ground ginger
75 g butter, melted

### CAKE
125 g butter, softened
1 cup caster sugar
2 eggs
1 teaspoon vanilla essence
2 cups Champion standard grade flour
1 teaspoon Edmonds baking powder
1 teaspoon Edmonds baking soda
  dissolved in ¾ cup warm milk
½ cup (125 g) sour cream

To make the topping, combine all ingredients in a bowl. Mix well. To make the cake, cream butter and sugar until light and fluffy. Add eggs one at a time, beating well after each addition. Beat in essence. Sift flour and baking powder. Fold flour, milk and sour cream alternately into creamed mixture. Spoon into a greased 22-cm-diameter cake tin that has had the base lined with baking paper. Spoon topping evenly over cake, then gently press onto cake. Bake at 180°C for 1 hour or until a skewer inserted in centre of cake comes out clean. Leave in tin for 10 minutes before transferring to a wire rack to cool. *(Above right)*

# SPICED FEIJOA CAKE

175 g butter, softened
1 cup caster sugar
3 eggs
1 teaspoon vanilla essence
1 cup chopped peeled feijoas
¼ cup chopped crystallised ginger
2½ cups Champion standard
   grade flour

2 teaspoons Edmonds baking powder
½ teaspoon Edmonds baking soda
2 teaspoons ground ginger
1 cup (250 g) sour cream
Cream Cheese Icing (see page 179)
chopped crystallised ginger to garnish

Cream butter and sugar until light and fluffy. Add eggs one at a time, beating well after each addition. Beat in essence. Fold in feijoas and crystallised ginger. Sift together flour, baking powder, baking soda and ground ginger. Fold into creamed mixture. Fold in sour cream. Transfer mixture to a 22-cm-diameter cake tin that has had the base lined with baking paper. Bake at 180°C for 65 minutes or until cake springs back when lightly pressed. Leave in tin for 10 minutes before transferring to a wire rack. When cake is cold, spread with Cream Cheese Icing. Garnish with crystallised ginger.

BISCUITS

# ALMOND CRESCENT BISCUITS

200 g butter, softened
1/2 cup caster sugar
1/2 teaspoon almond essence

1¼ cups Champion standard grade flour
70 g packet ground almonds
icing sugar to dust

Cream butter and sugar until light and fluffy. Beat in essence. Sift flour. Fold flour and ground almonds into creamed mixture. Spoon mixture into a piping bag fitted with a 1-cm-diameter star nozzle. Pipe small crescent shapes onto lightly greased oven trays. Bake at 160°C for 25 minutes. Cool biscuits on trays. Five minutes after removing from the oven, dust biscuits lightly with icing sugar. **Makes 38.** *(Below left)*

# ALMOND SHORTBREAD RINGS

250 g butter, softened
1 cup icing sugar
3–4 drops almond essence

1½ cups Champion standard grade flour
¾ cup Edmonds Fielder's cornflour
70 g packet ground almonds

Cream butter and icing sugar until light and fluffy. Add essence. Sift flour and cornflour. Stir into butter mixture along with ground almonds, mixing to a soft dough. Transfer dough to a lightly floured surface. Knead lightly for 2 minutes. Divide dough in half. Shape each portion into a ball and place in the centre of lightly greased oven trays. Pat or roll each ball into a circle about 20 cm in diameter. Using a sharp knife or pizza wheel, divide rounds into 8 equal portions, cutting almost right through the dough. Prick each section several times with a fork. Bake at 150°C for 40 minutes. Cool on a wire rack. To divide shortbread, break into sections along the marked lines. **Makes 16 portions.** *(Above right)*

# CHOCOLATE BROWNIE BISCUITS

*150 g dark chocolate, chopped*
*125 g butter, chopped*
*2 eggs*
*¾ cup caster sugar*
*2 teaspoons vanilla essence*

*1¼ cups Champion standard grade flour*
*¼ cup cocoa*
*½ teaspoon Edmonds baking powder*
*½ cup chopped walnuts*

Combine chocolate and butter in a saucepan. Stir constantly over a low heat until melted and smooth. Using an electric mixer, beat eggs, sugar and essence until thick and pale. Sift together flour, cocoa and baking powder. Fold chocolate mixture into egg mixture. Fold in dry ingredients and walnuts. Drop tablespoons of mixture onto greased oven trays. Bake at 180°C for 12 minutes. Transfer to wire racks to cool. **Makes 30.** *(Below left)*

# COFFEE KISSES

*250 g butter, softened*
*¾ cup icing sugar*
*3 teaspoons instant coffee powder*
*2 teaspoons milk*
*2 cups Champion standard grade flour*
*½ cup Edmonds Fielder's cornflour*

### COFFEE ICING

*1 cup icing sugar*
*1 teaspoon instant coffee powder*
*2 teaspoons melted butter*
*milk to mix*

Cream butter and icing sugar until light and fluffy. Dissolve coffee powder in milk. Add to creamed mixture and beat well. Sift flour and cornflour. Stir into creamed mixture. Spoon mixture into a piping bag fitted with a 2-cm-diameter star nozzle. Pipe 4-cm-diameter rosettes onto greased oven trays, allowing a little room for spreading. Bake at 180°C for 15–18 minutes. Cool on oven trays. Sandwich biscuits together with Coffee Icing. To make the icing, combine icing sugar and coffee in a bowl. Stir in butter and sufficient milk to mix to a spreadable consistency. **Makes 14.** *(Above right)*

# ESPRESSO BISCUITS WITH FUDGE FILLING

200 g butter, softened
¾ cup icing sugar
2 teaspoons instant espresso
 coffee powder
1 teaspoon hot water
1½ cups Champion standard
 grade flour

¾ cup Edmonds Fielder's cornflour
½ teaspoon Edmonds baking powder

### FUDGE FILLING
100 g dark chocolate, chopped
3 tablespoons butter
3 tablespoons icing sugar

Cream butter and icing sugar until light and fluffy. Dissolve coffee in the water. Add to creamed mixture and beat well. Sift flour, cornflour and baking powder. Add to creamed mixture. Mix well. Roll dough into small balls (the size of large marbles) and place on greased oven trays. Flatten slightly with the palm of your hand. Bake at 180°C for 20 minutes. Cool on wire racks. Sandwich 2 biscuits together with Fudge Filling. To make the Fudge Filling, combine chocolate and butter in a small saucepan. Stir constantly over a low heat until melted and smooth. Add icing sugar. Mix well. *Makes 24.* (Below left)

# GINGER BISCUITS

200 g butter, softened
¾ cup caster sugar
¼ cup golden syrup

2¼ cups Champion standard grade flour
2 teaspoons Edmonds baking soda
1 tablespoon ground ginger

Cream butter and caster sugar until light and fluffy. Add golden syrup and beat well. Sift dry ingredients. Stir into creamed mixture to form a soft dough. Roll heaped teaspoons of mixture into balls. Place 3–4 cm apart on greased oven trays. Flatten slightly with the palm of your hand. Bake at 160°C for 30 minutes. Cool on wire racks. *Makes 38.* (Above right)

# HAZELNUT SHORTBREAD FINGERS

250 g butter, softened
1 cup icing sugar
1 cup Edmonds Fielder's cornflour
1¾ cups Champion standard grade flour

½ cup chopped roasted hazelnuts
melted dark chocolate for dipping
  shortbread (optional)

Cream butter and icing sugar until light and fluffy. Sift together cornflour and flour. Mix sifted ingredients and hazelnuts into creamed mixture. Knead well. Divide dough into equal halves and form into logs 6 cm across and 2 cm in depth. Cover with plastic wrap and refrigerate for 45 minutes. Using a serrated knife, cut 1-cm-thick slices from the log. Place on greased oven trays. Prick with a fork. Bake at 160°C for 35–40 minutes or until pale golden. If desired, dip each shortbread finger into melted dark chocolate to half cover the shortbread. *Makes 40.* *(Below left)*

# MACADAMIA NUT AND WHITE CHOCOLATE BISCUITS

200 g butter, softened
1 cup caster sugar
2 eggs
1 teaspoon vanilla essence

3 cups Champion standard grade flour
2 teaspoons Edmonds baking powder
100 g chopped white chocolate
⅓ cup chopped macadamia nuts

Cream butter and caster sugar until light and fluffy. Add eggs one at a time, beating well after each addition. Beat in essence. Sift flour and baking powder. Stir into creamed mixture along with chocolate and nuts. Take heaped teaspoons of mixture and roll into balls. Place on greased oven trays, allowing room for spreading. Flatten slightly with a floured fork. Bake at 180°C for 15–18 minutes until golden. Cool on wire racks. *Makes 40.* *(Above right)*

# ORANGE MELTING MOMENTS

200 g butter, softened
¾ cup icing sugar
finely grated zest of 1 medium orange
1 cup Champion standard grade flour
1 cup Edmonds Fielder's cornflour
½ teaspoon Edmonds baking powder

ORANGE ICING

1 cup icing sugar
1 teaspoon butter
1 tablespoon freshly
   squeezed orange juice
a little boiling water to mix

Cream butter and icing sugar until light and fluffy. Beat in orange zest. Sift flour, cornflour and baking powder. Add to creamed mixture. Mix well. Roll dough into small balls (the size of large marbles) and place on a greased oven tray. Flatten slightly with a floured fork. Bake at 180°C for 20 minutes. Cool on wire racks. Sandwich 2 biscuits together with Orange Icing. To make the Orange Icing, place icing sugar, butter and orange juice in a bowl. Add sufficient water to mix to a spreadable consistency. **Makes 22.** *(Below left)*

# YOGHURT RAISIN BISCUITS

125 g butter
½ cup sugar
1 egg
1 teaspoon vanilla essence

¾ cup yoghurt-covered raisins
2 cups Champion standard grade flour
1½ teaspoons Edmonds baking powder

Melt butter. Cool slightly. Using a wooden spoon, beat sugar and egg together for 2 minutes, until thick and pale. Add butter and mix well. Stir in essence and raisins. Sift flour and baking powder. Stir into liquid ingredients. Take heaped teaspoons of mixture and form into balls. Place 3–4 cm apart on greased oven trays. Flatten slightly with the palm of your hand. Bake at 180°C for 15 minutes until golden. Cool on wire racks. **Makes 25.** *(Above right)*

# SLICES

# APPLE SHORTCAKE SQUARES

4 apples, peeled and sliced
finely grated zest and juice of ½ lemon
1 tablespoon sugar
2 tablespoons water
2 cups Champion standard grade flour
1 teaspoon Edmonds baking powder

125 g butter
¼ cup sugar
1 egg, beaten
1 to 2 tablespoons milk
icing sugar to dust

Put apples, lemon zest and juice, first measure of sugar and water in saucepan and cook slowly until apples are soft. Sift flour and baking powder into a bowl. Cut in butter until it resembles coarse breadcrumbs. Mix in second measure of sugar and egg. Add sufficient milk to mix to a soft dough. Knead until smooth. Form into a ball and wrap in plastic wrap. Refrigerate for 30 minutes. Divide dough in half and roll out each piece to fit a greased 22-cm square cake tin. Place one piece of dough in tin and spread apple over it. Lightly press remaining dough on top. Bake at 180°C for 25 minutes. Cool. Dust with sifted icing sugar. Cut into squares. *(Top right)*

# APRICOT AND PISTACHIO NUT SLICE

### FILLING
400 g roughly chopped dried apricots
1 cup water
½ cup sugar
finely grated zest of 1 lemon
½ cup roughly chopped pistachio nuts

### OAT CRUMBLE
200 g butter, softened
1 cup lightly packed brown sugar
2 cups Champion standard grade flour
1 teaspoon Edmonds baking powder
1 teaspoon ground ginger
2 cups Fleming's rolled oats

To make the filling, place apricots, water, sugar and lemon zest in a saucepan. Cook over a low heat for about 15 minutes until all the liquid is absorbed and the apricots are soft. Remove from heat. Cool. Stir in nuts. For the oat crumble base, cream butter and sugar until light and fluffy. Sift together flour, baking powder and ginger. Add to creamed mixture, along with the rolled oats. Mix well. Press three-quarters of the oat crumble over the base of a greased 20 x 30 cm shallow baking tin that has had the base lined with baking paper. Spread apricot filling over the base, then sprinkle remaining oat mixture over top. Use the back of a spoon to lightly press topping into filling. Bake at 180°C for 40 minutes until golden. Cool in tin before cutting. *(Middle right)*

# CARAMEL DATE FINGERS

| FILLING | BASE |
| --- | --- |
| 1 cup pitted dates, chopped | 125 g butter |
| 1 cup water | 1/2 cup sugar |
| 1 tablespoon brown sugar | 1 egg |
| 1 teaspoon butter | 1¾ cups Champion standard grade flour |
| 2 teaspoons cocoa | 1 teaspoon Edmonds baking powder |
| 1/4 teaspoon vanilla essence | |

To make the filling, combine dates, water, sugar, butter and cocoa in a saucepan. Cook gently over a low heat, stirring frequently, until a paste-like consistency is obtained. Add essence. Cool. For the base, cream butter and sugar until light and fluffy. Add egg and beat well. Sift flour and baking powder together. Stir into creamed mixture. Press out half the mixture to fit the base of a greased 20-cm square tin. Spread with date mixture. Crumble remaining base mixture over filling. Press lightly with the back of a spoon. Bake at 180°C for 30 minutes or until golden. Cut into fingers. *(Below left)*

N.B. Other dried fruits such as prunes, apricots and raisins, alone or mixed, can replace dates.

# COCONUT CHOCOLATE BROWNIES

| | |
| --- | --- |
| 125 g butter | 1/2 cup coconut |
| 1/4 cup cocoa | 1/2 cup Champion standard grade flour |
| 1 cup sugar | 1/2 teaspoon Edmonds baking powder |
| 2 eggs | icing sugar to dust |
| 1 teaspoon vanilla essence | |

Melt butter in a medium-sized saucepan. Add cocoa. Stir over a low heat for 1 minute. Remove from heat. Stir in sugar. Add eggs one at a time, beating well after each addition. Beat in essence and coconut. Sift flour and baking powder. Stir into mixture. Pour into a greased and lined shallow 20-cm square cake tin. Bake at 180°C for 30–35 minutes. Leave in tin for 5 minutes before turning out onto a wire rack. Cut into bars when cold. Dust with icing sugar. *(Above right)*

# COCONUT AND ALMOND SLICE

250 g packet plain sweet biscuits, crushed
¾ cup chopped toasted blanched almonds
1 cup coconut
finely grated zest and juice of 1 lemon
2 drops almond essence
100 g butter
½ cup sweetened condensed milk

### LEMON ICING

1½ cups icing sugar
2 tablespoons butter
1 teaspoon lemon juice
boiling water to mix

Combine biscuit crumbs, almonds, coconut, lemon zest, juice and essence in a bowl. Place butter and condensed milk in a small saucepan. Stir over a low heat until the butter melts. Pour over biscuit mixture. Mix well. Press over the base of a 20 x 25 cm shallow baking dish. Refrigerate for 1 hour until firm. To make the icing, combine all ingredients in a bowl, adding sufficient boiling water to mix to a stiff paste. Spread over slice. Refrigerate for 1 hour or until set. Store in the refrigerator.

# COFFEE OAT SLICE

### BASE
175 g butter, softened
½ cup caster sugar
1¾ cups Champion standard grade flour

### COFFEE FILLING
397 g can sweetened condensed milk
50 g butter
3 teaspoons instant coffee powder

### OAT TOPPING
1 cup Fleming's rolled oats
1 cup coarse coconut
50 g butter, melted
2 tablespoons golden syrup

To make the base, cream butter and sugar until light and fluffy. Add flour. Mix to a soft dough. Press over the base of a greased 20 x 30 cm shallow baking tin that has had the base lined with baking paper. Bake at 180°C for 15 minutes until light golden. Cool slightly. For the filling, place all ingredients in a small saucepan. Stir over a low heat until butter has melted and mixture is smooth. Bring to the boil, stirring constantly. Spread over partially cooked base. To make the topping, combine all ingredients in a bowl. Mix well. Sprinkle over coffee filling. Bake at 180°C for a further 15 minutes until golden. Cool in tin before cutting.

# COFFEE WALNUT SLICE

### BASE
175 g butter, softened
1 egg
2 cups Champion standard grade flour
½ cup caster sugar
¾ teaspoon Edmonds baking powder

### FILLING
397 g can sweetened condensed milk
2 tablespoons butter

2 tablespoons golden syrup
2 teaspoons coffee and chicory essence
¾ cup roughly chopped walnuts

### TOPPING
125 g butter, softened
½ cup caster sugar
1 cup Champion standard grade flour
1 teaspoon cinnamon

To make the base, beat butter, egg, flour, caster sugar and baking powder to a soft dough using an electric mixer. Press over the base of a greased shallow 25-cm square baking tin. Prick all over with a fork. Bake at 180°C for 20–25 minutes until golden. Next, prepare the filling. Place all filling ingredients in a saucepan. Stir over a low heat for 4–5 minutes until the mixture thickens. Remove from heat. Cool slightly. To make topping, beat all ingredients together for 1 minute with an electric mixer. Form into a ball and cover with plastic wrap. Refrigerate for at least 10 minutes. Spread cooled filling over cooked base. Coarsely grate topping dough over filling. Bake for 25–30 minutes until golden. Cool before cutting into slices. *(Below left)*

# HONEY NUT BARS

### BASE
1½ cups Champion standard
   grade flour
½ teaspoon Edmonds baking powder
¼ cup icing sugar
150 g butter, softened
2 egg yolks

### TOPPING
75 g butter
⅓ cup liquid honey
⅓ cup sugar
¾ cup hazelnuts
½ cup each blanched almonds,
   walnut pieces, pecan nuts

To make the base, place flour, baking powder, icing sugar and butter in a food processor. Pulse until mixture is crumbly. Add egg yolks and pulse until mixture comes together. Press over the base of an 18 x 27 cm shallow baking tin lined with baking paper and greased. Prick several times with a fork. Bake at 180°C for 15 minutes. To make the topping, place butter, honey and sugar in a saucepan. Stir over a low heat until mixture boils. Simmer for 2 minutes. Remove from heat and stir in nuts. Spread warm topping evenly over base. Bake for 20 minutes at 180°C. Cool, then cut into bars. Refrigerate during warmer weather. *(Above right)*

# NUTTY CRUNCH SLICE

1 cup sesame seeds
1 cup pumpkin kernels
1 cup coconut
1 cup chopped Brazil nuts
250 g packet gingernut biscuits

½ cup chopped dried apricots
1 teaspoon ground ginger
125 g butter
½ cup sweetened condensed milk

Combine sesame seeds, pumpkin kernels, coconut and nuts in a frying pan. Stir continuously over a low–medium heat for 6–8 minutes until mixture starts to pop and the coconut turns a light golden colour. Transfer mixture to a bowl. Crush gingernuts to a fine crumb in a food processor. Stir crumbs, apricots and ginger into toasted mixture. Place butter and condensed milk in a small saucepan. Stir over a low heat until butter has melted. Pour over dry ingredients and mix well. Press mixture over the base of a lightly greased 20 x 30 cm shallow baking tin. Cover and refrigerate for 1 hour before cutting. Cover again and store in the refrigerator.

# OATY DATE BARS

### FILLING
*2 cups pitted, chopped dates*
*¼ cup water*
*¼ cup lemon juice*

### BASE
*125 g butter, softened*
*¾ cup brown sugar*

*1 egg*
*1 tablespoon golden syrup*
*1 teaspoon vanilla essence*
*1¼ cups Champion wholemeal flour*
*1 teaspoon Edmonds baking powder*
*1 cup Fleming's rolled oats*
*1 cup coconut*

To make the filling, combine dates, water and lemon juice in a saucepan. Cook over a low heat, stirring frequently, until dates are soft and all the liquid is absorbed. Cool. To make the base, cream butter and sugar until light and fluffy. Add egg and beat well. Beat in golden syrup and essence. Add flour, baking powder, rolled oats and coconut to creamed mixture. Mix well. Divide dough into 2 equal portions. Press one portion over the base of a greased 20 x 30 cm shallow baking tin. Spread filling over top. Dot small pieces of dough over filling and carefully spread together to form a top layer. Bake at 180°C for 25–30 minutes, until golden. Cool before cutting into fingers.

# ROCKY ROAD SLICE

### BASE

1 cup Champion standard grade flour
½ teaspoon Edmonds baking powder
3 tablespoons cocoa
¾ cup caster sugar
¾ cup coconut
125 g butter, melted
1 egg

### TOPPING

250 g dark chocolate, chopped (or melts)
2 tablespoons Kremelta
25 marshmallows
½ cup toasted coconut
½ cup pistachio nuts
    (or chopped walnuts)

Sift flour, baking powder and cocoa into a bowl. Stir in caster sugar and coconut. Add butter and egg and mix well. Spread over the base of a greased 18 x 27 cm shallow baking tin. Bake at 180°C for 20–25 minutes. Cool for 15 minutes, then spread with topping. To make the topping, place chocolate and Kremelta in a heatproof bowl and set over a saucepan of simmering water. Stir continuously until chocolate and Kremelta have melted and the mixture is smooth. Set aside for 5 minutes to cool slightly. Add marshmallows, coconut and nuts to melted chocolate. Mix well. Spread over warm base. Allow topping to set before cutting into pieces.

    N.B. During warm weather, refrigerate slice for setting and keep in the refrigerator.

# WHITE AND DARK CHOCOLATE BROWNIE SLICE

200 g butter, softened
1 cup sugar
3 eggs
½ cup cocoa
1 cup Champion standard grade flour

¼ teaspoon Edmonds baking powder
100 g white chocolate, roughly chopped
¾ cup (75 g) chopped walnuts
⅓ cup milk
icing sugar to dust

Cream butter and sugar until light and fluffy. Add eggs one at a time, beating well after each addition. Sift together cocoa, flour and baking powder. Fold dry ingredients, chocolate, walnuts and milk into creamed mixture. Transfer to a thoroughly greased 20-cm square shallow cake tin. Bake at 150°C for about 50 minutes — the brownies should be a little sticky. Cool before cutting into squares. Dust with icing sugar.

# MUFFINS, LOAVES AND TARTLETS

# FETA AND PARSLEY MUFFINS

150 g butter
2 cups milk
2 eggs
3½ cups Champion standard
   grade flour

3 teaspoons Edmonds baking powder
¼ teaspoon cayenne pepper
100 g feta cheese, diced
1 cup grated tasty cheddar cheese
3 tablespoons chopped parsley

Combine butter and milk in a small saucepan. Stir over a low heat until butter has melted. Remove from heat. Set aside to cool slightly. Whisk in eggs. Sift flour, baking powder and cayenne into a bowl. Stir in cheeses and parsley. Add liquid ingredients, stirring until just combined. Do not overmix. Divide mixture between 12 greased deep muffin tins. Bake at 200°C for 20–25 minutes until muffins are risen and golden. Leave in tins for 5 minutes. *Makes 12.*
*(Below left)*

# TINY CHEESE MUFFINS

50 g butter
¾ cup milk
1 egg
1½ cups Champion standard
   grade flour

1½ teaspoons Edmonds baking powder
¼ teaspoon salt
¾ cup grated tasty cheddar cheese
1 tablespoon chopped parsley (optional)

Place butter and milk in a small saucepan. Stir over a low heat until butter has melted. Remove from heat and cool for 5 minutes. Whisk in egg. Sift flour, baking powder and salt. Stir in cheese and parsley. Stir liquid ingredients into flour, mixing just until combined — do not overmix. Spoon mixture into 18 greased tiny muffin tins. Bake at 200°C for 12 minutes until risen and golden. Cool in tins for 5 minutes before removing. *Makes 18.* *(Above right)*
   N.B. This mixture can also be cooked in 6 regular muffin tins. Bake for 15 minutes.

# FRESH LEMON LOAF

125 g butter, softened
¾ cup sugar
1 teaspoon grated lemon zest
2 eggs
2 cups Champion self-raising flour
¼ teaspoon salt
½ cup milk
¼ cup chopped walnuts

GLAZE
¼ cup lemon juice
¼ cup sugar

Cream butter, sugar and lemon zest until light and fluffy. Add eggs one at a time, beating well after each addition. Sift flour and salt. Fold into creamed mixture alternately with milk. Fold in walnuts. Transfer to a greased and lined 22 cm loaf tin. Bake at 180°C for 45–50 minutes or until loaf springs back when lightly touched. While loaf is hot, pour over glaze. Cool in tin. To make the glaze, place lemon juice and sugar in a small saucepan. Stir over a low heat until sugar dissolves. Bring to the boil. Remove from heat. Cool. *(Below left)*

# GINGERBREAD LOAF

2 cups Champion standard grade flour
pinch of salt
1 tablespoon ground ginger
1 tablespoon cinnamon
2 eggs
½ cup sugar

100 g butter
2 tablespoons golden syrup
1½ teaspoons Edmonds baking soda
¾ cup natural unsweetened yoghurt
½ cup sultanas

Sift flour, salt, ginger and cinnamon into a bowl. In a separate bowl beat eggs and sugar until thick and pale. Melt together butter and golden syrup and cool slightly. Add to egg and sugar mixture. Fold in dry ingredients. In a small bowl dissolve baking soda in the yoghurt. Stir into the loaf mixture with sultanas until well combined. Spoon into a greased and lined 22 cm loaf tin. Bake at 180°C for 45–50 minutes. Leave in tin for 10 minutes before turning out onto a wire rack.
*(Above right)*

# FRUIT TARTLETS

*Sweet Shortcrust Pastry (see page 180)*

### FILLING

3 tablespoons Edmonds custard powder
1 cup milk
2 egg yolks
2 tablespoons sugar
2 tablespoons brandy
¹/₂ cup cream, whipped

### TOPPING

*fresh or tinned fruit, e.g. grapes, melon,
strawberries, kiwifruit, diced or sliced*

### GLAZE

¹/₄ cup apricot jam
2 teaspoons water

Roll the chilled pastry out on a lightly floured surface to a thickness of 4 mm. Using a 7-cm-round fluted biscuit cutter, stamp circles from the dough. Line eighteen 7-cm-diameter tartlet tins. Prick the bases of pastry cases. Refrigerate for 10 minutes, then freeze for 5 minutes. Bake at 180°C for 12–15 minutes until golden. Cool. To make filling, mix custard powder to a smooth paste with a little of the milk. Whisk in remaining milk, yolks and sugar. Cook over a low heat, stirring constantly until the mixture thickens. Do not allow to boil. Stir in the brandy. Cover the surface of filling directly with plastic wrap to prevent skin forming. Cool for 1 hour. Fold in cream. Spoon filling into the prepared tartlet cases. Arrange the fruit on top of the custard. To make the glaze, gently heat together jam and water. Sieve. Spoon or brush glaze over the fruit. *Makes 18.*

# MINI PECAN TARTLETS

### PASTRY
3/4 cup Champion standard grade flour
50 g butter
2 tablespoons sugar
1 egg yolk

### FILLING
1/4 cup brown sugar

1/4 cup golden syrup
1/4 cup cream
2 eggs
1/4 cup chopped pecan nuts

24 pecan nuts to garnish
icing sugar to dust

To make the pastry, sift flour. Cut in butter until it resembles fine breadcrumbs. Stir in sugar. Add egg yolk. Mix to a stiff dough. Chill for 30 minutes before using. Roll pastry out to a thickness of 3 mm. Using a 7-cm-diameter biscuit cutter, stamp shapes from pastry. Use pastry to line 24 mini muffin tins. Place muffin tins in the freezer while preparing the filling. Combine brown sugar, golden syrup and cream in a small saucepan. Stir over a low heat for 1–2 minutes until mixture is smooth. Remove from heat. Stir in eggs and chopped pecan nuts. Half fill pastry cases with mixture. Place a nut on top of each tartlet. Bake at 180°C for 12–15 minutes until the filling is set and the tartlets are golden. Just before serving, dust with icing sugar. **Makes 24.** (Below left)

# TINY LEMON CURD TARTLETS

### LEMON CURD FILLING
1 tablespoon finely grated lemon zest
1/4 cup lemon juice
2 eggs, lightly beaten
50 g butter
1/4 cup caster sugar

### PASTRY
100 g butter, softened
1/4 cup caster sugar
1 egg yolk
1 cup Champion standard grade flour

To make the Lemon Curd Filling, combine lemon zest and juice, eggs, butter and sugar in the top of a double boiler or in a heatproof bowl set over simmering water. Stir constantly until sugar dissolves and curd thickens. Remove from heat. Cover and cool. For the pastry, cream butter and sugar until light and fluffy. Add egg yolk and beat well. Stir in flour. Gather pastry into a ball and wrap in plastic wrap. Refrigerate for 20 minutes. Roll pastry out on a lightly floured surface to a thickness of 2–3 mm. Using a 7-cm-diameter biscuit cutter, cut circles from pastry. Transfer to mini muffin tins. Prick bases with a fork. Freeze for 5 minutes. Bake at 180°C for 10 minutes until golden. Remove pastry cases from tins and cool on a wire rack. Just before serving, fill with lemon curd. **Makes 24.** (Above right)

# FINGER FOODS

# ANTIPASTO

Antipasto is an Italian term for "before the meal" and can include any of the following types of finger foods — hummus, olives, sliced meats such as salami, prosciutto, smoked pork or beef, semi-dried tomatoes, feta cheese marinated in olive oil and rosemary sprigs, roasted capsicums, canned artichoke hearts, cherry tomatoes. The following recipes from the Preserves section of this book can be included on an antipasto platter — Chargrilled Capsicums with Garlic and Rosemary (see page 172), Marinated Olives with Herbs (see page 174) and Oven-dried Tomatoes (see page 175). Accompany an antipasto platter with fresh crusty bread or Crostini (see below). *(Middle left)*

# BLUE CHEESE SPREAD

250 g blue cheese
150 g cream cheese
1 small onion, chopped
2 tablespoons softened butter
1 tablespoon Worcestershire sauce

dash Tabasco sauce
2 tablespoons dry sherry
pumpernickel bread and Crostini
   (see below), to serve
tiny sprigs of fresh herbs to garnish

Crumble blue cheese into the bowl of a food processor. Add cream cheese, onion, butter, Worcestershire and Tabasco sauces and sherry. Process until smooth. Transfer to a bowl. Cover and refrigerate until firm. When ready to use, spread on pumpernickel bread or crostini. Garnish with sprigs of fresh herbs. *(Below)*

### CROSTINI

Cut a **French loaf** into 4-mm-thick slices. Brush both sides of bread with **olive oil**. Place in a single layer on a baking tray. Bake at 190°C for 10–12 minutes, until golden. Cool. Store in an airtight container until required. Stored thus, crostini will keep for up to 1 week. *(Below)*

# CHEESE BALL

250 g cream cheese
1 cup grated tasty cheddar cheese
1 pickled onion, finely chopped
2 tablespoons finely chopped parsley
2 tablespoons finely chopped gherkin
1 tablespoon tomato sauce

1 teaspoon Worcestershire sauce
few drops Tabasco sauce
¼ teaspoon paprika
½ cup chopped walnuts, approximately
crackers or sliced fresh bread to serve

Combine cheeses in a bowl. Add pickled onion, parsley, gherkin, tomato, Worcestershire and Tabasco sauces and paprika. Beat well to combine. Shape into a ball. Roll in chopped walnuts until well coated. Wrap and chill until firm. Serve with crackers or sliced fresh bread. *(Top right)*

# DEVILLED ALMONDS

2 tablespoons oil
2 cups blanched almonds

¼ teaspoon chilli powder, approximately
2 teaspoons salt

Heat oil in a frying pan. Add almonds and stir continuously until golden. Drain almonds on paper towels. Combine chilli and salt. Toss almonds in this mixture to coat. Leave to dry. **Makes 2 cups.** *(Top left)*

# FELAFEL WITH YOGHURT SAUCE

### YOGHURT SAUCE

1 cup natural unsweetened yoghurt
1 clove garlic, crushed
1 tablespoon chopped parsley
1 tablespoon tahini
¼ teaspoon ground cumin
freshly ground black pepper to season

### FELAFEL

2 x 300 g cans chickpeas in brine
1 stalk celery, chopped

1 onion, chopped
1 teaspoon crushed garlic
2 tablespoons Champion standard
   grade flour
2 tablespoons tahini
1 teaspoon ground cumin
½ teaspoon turmeric
½ teaspoon salt
freshly ground black pepper to season
Champion standard grade flour to coat
vegetable oil to cook

To make the yoghurt sauce, combine all ingredients. Mix well. Cover and refrigerate until required. To make the felafel, place chickpeas, celery, onion, garlic, flour, tahini, cumin, turmeric, salt and pepper in a food processor. Blend to a coarse consistency. Transfer to a bowl. Cover and refrigerate for 1 hour. Spread a little flour onto a flat plate. Take large teaspoonfuls of mixture and roll into balls, then flatten slightly with the palm of the hand to make a little patty. Roll in flour to lightly coat. Pour oil into a frying pan to a level of 1 cm. Heat pan. Cook felafels for about 5 minutes, or until golden, turning once. Drain on paper towels. Serve with Yoghurt Sauce. **Makes 36.** *(Below)*

# MIXED SATAYS WITH PEANUT DIP

350 g piece fast-fry steak, e.g. rump,
   porterhouse, fillet
350 g boneless, skinless chicken (2
   chicken breasts)
18 shelled raw king prawns
18 x 20-cm-long wooden skewers
Quick Peanut Dip (see page 54)

### MARINADE

¾ cup coconut milk
3 tablespoons soy sauce
3 tablespoons vegetable oil
3 cloves garlic, crushed
1 teaspoon ground cumin
1 teaspoon ground coriander

Remove any visible fat from the steak and chicken. Cut lengthwise into thin strips. Place beef, chicken, and prawns in individual bowls. Make marinade by combining all ingredients. Divide marinade between the 3 bowls. Cover and refrigerate for 1–2 hours. Soak skewers in cold water for 30 minutes to prevent burning while cooking. Thread beef onto 6 skewers and chicken onto 6 skewers. Thread 3 prawns onto each of the remaining 6 skewers. Place beef and chicken skewers in a single layer on a baking tray. Preheat oven grill. Grill for 6–8 minutes, turning occasionally, then add prawn skewers and cook for a further 4–6 minutes until cooked through. Serve with Quick Peanut Dip. **Makes 18.** *(Top)*

# GUACAMOLE

1 ripe avocado
1/2 cup sour cream
2 teaspoons lemon juice
few drops Tabasco sauce

1/4 – 1/2 teaspoon chilli powder
salt to season
sprig of fresh herbs to garnish (optional)

Remove flesh from avocado and mash. Mix in sour cream, lemon juice, Tabasco sauce and chilli powder. Season with salt to taste. Cover. Chill until ready to serve. Garnish with a sprig of fresh herbs. **Makes about 1 cup.** (Below left)

# PARMESAN AND GARLIC TWISTS

### DOUGH
1 1/2 teaspoons sugar
300 ml warm water
1 tablespoon Edmonds active yeast
3 cups Champion high grade flour
1 1/2 teaspoons salt
2 tablespoons olive oil

### TOPPING
2 tablespoons olive oil
1 clove garlic, crushed
2–3 tablespoons freshly
    grated parmesan cheese
1 tablespoon finely chopped rosemary
rock salt to sprinkle (optional)

Dissolve the sugar in warm water. Sprinkle the yeast over the water and set aside in a warm place for 10 minutes until frothy. Combine the flour and salt in a large bowl. Stir in frothy yeast mixture and oil. Mix to a soft dough. Transfer the dough to a liberally floured surface and knead for 5 minutes until smooth and elastic. Divide the dough into 8 equal portions. To make each twist, take a portion of the dough and divide in half. Roll each piece into a 20-cm-long sausage shape. Twist the dough lengths together by using a dab of olive oil at the join and squeezing the dough ends to secure. Place the twists on a lightly greased oven tray, allowing room for spreading. To make the topping, combine oil and garlic. Brush the twists with the oil and garlic topping. Cover with plastic wrap and sit in a warm place for about 45 minutes until well risen. Sprinkle with parmesan cheese, rosemary and rock salt. Bake at 220°C for 10 minutes, then reduce temperature to 200°C and bake for a further 5 minutes until golden. **Makes 8.** (Above right)

# PROSCIUTTO-WRAPPED ASPARAGUS

*36 slender asparagus spears*
*a little olive oil to brush*

*6 slices prosciutto, halved lengthwise*
*Hollandaise Sauce (see page 182) to serve*

Trim asparagus spears to an even length, removing the woody ends. Blanch asparagus in boiling water, or microwave until just tender. Drain in a sieve under cold running water to refresh. Drain thoroughly. Lay on a double thickness of paper towels, then pat dry with more paper towels. Brush spears lightly with a little olive oil. Bundle together 3 spears and wrap a strip of prosciutto around each bundle. Arrange on a serving plate. Serve accompanied by Hollandaise Sauce. *Makes 12 bundles.*

# QUICK PEANUT DIP

1 teaspoon oil
1 small onion, finely chopped
1 cup crunchy peanut butter

¾ cup milk (or coconut milk)
1 tablespoon chilli sauce (optional)

Heat oil in a small saucepan. Cook onion for 4–5 minutes until soft. Add remaining ingredients to the pan. Stir over a low heat for 3–4 minutes until mixture is smooth and heated through. For a delicious snack, serve warm. Accompany with vegetable sticks or pita crisps.

# SESAME CHICKEN STICKS

*2 skinless boneless chicken breasts*
*1 tablespoon soy sauce*
*1 teaspoon oil*

*¾ cup sesame seeds*
*chilli sauce to serve*

Cut chicken into 1.5-cm-wide strips. Combine chicken, soy sauce and oil in a bowl. Mix well. Cover and refrigerate for at least 30 minutes. Place sesame seeds on a flat plate. Roll chicken sticks in the sesame seeds to cover. Transfer to a lightly oiled roasting dish. Bake at 220°C for 15 minutes until cooked through and golden, turning every 3–4 minutes. Serve hot, accompanied by a small bowl of chilli sauce. *(Below left)*

N.B. If desired, serve Sesame Chicken Sticks with Quick Peanut Dip (see opposite).

# SESAME-MARINATED CHICKEN NIBBLES

*¼ cup liquid honey*
*¼ cup hoisin sauce*
*3 tablespoons sesame seeds*
*2 tablespoons tomato sauce*
*2 tablespoons dry sherry*

*1 tablespoon sesame oil*
*1 tablespoon soy sauce*
*2 cloves garlic, crushed*
*750 g chicken nibbles*

In a small bowl combine all ingredients except chicken nibbles. Mix well. Place chicken nibbles in a medium bowl. Pour over marinade. Toss nibbles until evenly coated. Cover and refrigerate for at least 2 hours, or up to 8 hours. Place nibbles in a shallow roasting dish. Bake at 200°C for 20 minutes, turning occasionally, until golden and cooked through. *(Above right)*

# SPICY CAJUN POTATO WEDGES

*3 tablespoons Champion standard
   grade flour
3 teaspoons Cajun spice mix
½ teaspoon chilli powder*

*6 medium potatoes, washed
oil to coat
sour cream to serve
paprika to garnish*

Combine flour, Cajun spice mix and chilli powder. Place in a plastic bag. Cut potatoes in half lengthwise, then cut each half into 4 wedges. Place wedges in a bowl. Pour over just enough oil to lightly coat the potatoes once tossed thoroughly. Transfer wedges to the plastic bag. Twist top of bag and shake vigorously to coat. Preheat oven to 220°C, placing a large roasting dish in the oven to heat. Add wedges. Bake for 40 minutes, turning occasionally, until potatoes are cooked through and golden. Accompany with sour cream that has been lightly sprinkled with paprika. ***Serves 4 as a snack.*** *(Middle right)*

# SPRING ROLLS WITH CHILLI DIPPING SAUCE

### CHILLI DIPPING SAUCE

*¼ cup rice wine vinegar
1 tablespoon sweet chilli sauce
1 tablespoon brown sugar
1 teaspoon grated root ginger*

### SPRING ROLLS

*100 g vermicelli noodles
1 tablespoon vegetable oil
300 g lean pork mince
2 cloves garlic, crushed*

*1 tablespoon finely grated root ginger
2 spring onions, finely chopped
3 tablespoons sweet chilli sauce
1 tablespoon fish sauce
2 tablespoons chopped coriander
1 tablespoon Edmonds
   Fielder's cornflour
2 tablespoons water
20 spring roll wrappers
vegetable oil to cook*

To make the dipping sauce, combine all ingredients. Mix well. To make the spring rolls, place vermicelli in a bowl. Pour over warm water to cover. Stand for 10 minutes. Drain, then roughly chop. Heat oil in a frying pan. Cook pork, garlic and ginger for 2 minutes, stirring often, until pork is cooked. Add vermicelli, spring onions, chilli sauce, fish sauce and coriander. Cook for 1–2 minutes until combined. Set aside to cool. Mix cornflour to a paste with water. Take one spring roll wrapper at a time. Brush edges lightly with cornflour paste. Place a tablespoonful of mixture along one edge of the wrapper, leaving a 1.5 cm border for folding over filling. Fold edges in and roll up to enclose. Pour oil into a saucepan to a level of 5 cm. Heat. Cook spring rolls for 1–2 minutes, or until golden, removing with a slotted spoon as they are ready. Drain on paper towels. Place dipping sauce in a small dish in the middle of a platter. Pile spring rolls onto platter and serve immediately. ***Makes 20.*** *(Top left)*

# SUSHI

*2 cups short grain rice*
*3 cups cold water*
*⅓ cup sugar*
*⅓ cup rice vinegar*
*1 level tablespoon salt*
*7 toasted nori sheets*
*2 teaspoons wasabi paste*

## FILLING COMBINATIONS (ALL FINELY SLICED INTO STRIPS)
*— pickled ginger, telegraph cucumber and red capsicum*
*— smoked salmon, telegraph cucumber and yellow capsicum*
*— carrot, telegraph cucumber and red capsicum*

## DIPPING SAUCE
*3 tablespoons light soy sauce*
*¼ teaspoon wasabi paste*

Place rice in a sieve. Rinse thoroughly under cold running water. Place rice and water in a saucepan. Set aside for 30 minutes. Cover pan and bring to the boil over a high heat. Reduce heat to very low and simmer for about 15 minutes — until all the water has been absorbed. Turn off heat and stand for 15 minutes. Combine sugar, vinegar and salt. Gradually add to the rice, tossing rice with a fork. Cover and set aside for 10 minutes to cool slightly. Divide into 7 equal portions. To assemble, place a sheet of nori, rough side up, on a damp bamboo sushi mat. Spread one portion of rice over the nori. Using the wasabi paste sparingly, spread a narrow line across one end of the rice, 2.5 cm from the edge. Arrange filling ingredients of choice along the line of wasabi. Starting at the edge with the filling, use the bamboo mat to help roll the sushi into a tight log, pressing down firmly as you roll. Using a sharp knife, trim off ends, then cut log into 5 equal portions. To make the dipping sauce, combine soy sauce and wasabi paste. Transfer to a serving dish. *Makes 35 pieces.*

# LIGHT MEALS
# AND SALADS

# LIGHT
# MEALS

# CHICKEN ENCHILADAS

400 g can tomatoes in juice
113 g can jalapeño peppers
1 teaspoon ground coriander
½ teaspoon salt
250 g sour cream
2 tablespoons oil

2 cups chopped cooked chicken
1 small onion, finely chopped
salt and freshly ground black pepper
8 x 20-cm-diameter flour tortillas
¾ cup grated tasty cheddar cheese

Put tomatoes in juice, jalapeño peppers, coriander and salt into a food processor or blender. Process until smooth. Add sour cream and process to combine. Set aside. Heat oil in a saucepan. Add chicken and onion. Cook for about 5 minutes, stirring constantly, until onion is soft. Season to taste with salt and pepper. Lay tortillas on a flat surface. Spread with tomato mixture. Divide chicken mixture between the tortillas, spreading in a log shape along one edge. Roll up like a sponge roll. Place seam side down in ovenproof dish. Repeat with remaining tortillas and chicken. Pour remaining tomato mixture over. Sprinkle with cheese. Cover dish with lid or foil. Cook at 180°C for 30 minutes. Remove lid, then grill until golden. **Serves 4.** *(Below left)*

# CRISPY-SKINNED POTATOES WITH BACON AND AVOCADO FILLING

4 potatoes, washed
oil to brush
knob of butter
1 tablespoon oil
4 rashers rindless bacon, chopped

1 firm, ripe avocado
2 spring onions, chopped
¾ cup grated tasty cheddar cheese
salt and freshly ground black pepper

Lightly brush potatoes with oil. Bake at 180°C for 1–1½ hours until potatoes are tender when pierced with a sharp knife. Cut potatoes in half lengthwise. Scoop out flesh, leaving a 5-mm-thick potato shell. Place potato flesh in a bowl. Brush inside of potato shells lightly with oil. Place on a baking tray. Bake at 250°C for 12–15 minutes until golden. Add butter to potato flesh and mash to a smooth consistency. Heat oil in a frying pan. Cook bacon until beginning to crisp. Cut avocado in half. Remove stone. Peel, then dice. Add bacon, avocado, spring onions and cheese to potato. Season to taste with salt and pepper. Pile filling back into the shells. Bake at 200°C for 20 minutes to heat through. **Serves 4.** *(Above right)*

# CURRIED VEGETABLE PARCELS

2 tablespoons oil
2 cups small cauliflower florets
2 cups peeled, seeded and
  finely diced pumpkin
1 onion, chopped
1 courgette, thinly sliced
1 red capsicum, seeded and sliced
1 green capsicum, seeded and sliced

1 tablespoon curry powder
1 teaspoon crushed garlic
6 tablespoons coconut-milk powder
½ cup warm water
18 sheets filo pastry
50 g butter, melted
relish or chutney to serve

Heat the oil in a heavy-based frying pan. Cook all the vegetables and the curry powder for 5 minutes over a low–medium heat, stirring frequently. Cover the pan and cook for about 10 minutes, stirring occasionally, until the vegetables are tender. Add the garlic. Mix the coconut-milk powder and water to a smooth paste. Add to the pan, stirring well. Simmer, uncovered, for 6–8 minutes or until the sauce is thick. Cool. For each parcel, lay a sheet of filo pastry on a flat surface. Brush with melted butter. Layer 2 more sheets of the pastry on top, brushing between each sheet with butter. Fold pastry in half widthways. Spoon one-sixth of the vegetable mixture in a line (about 8 cm long) along one long edge of the pastry. Roll up to form a log. Squeeze the pastry together around each end of the filling to form a cracker. Place the parcels on a greased baking tray. Brush with melted butter. Bake at 190°C for 12–15 minutes until golden. Serve immediately accompanied by relish or chutney. *Makes 6.*

# FETA, OLIVE AND SUNDRIED TOMATO CALZONE

### DOUGH

1¹/2 teaspoons sugar
300 ml warm water
2 tablespoons Edmonds active yeast
3 cups Champion high grade flour
1¹/2 teaspoons salt
¹/4 cup olive oil

### FILLING

75 g olive tapenade
100 g feta cheese, cut into 1 cm dice
2 roasted capsicums (see page 188
    for method), sliced
4 artichoke hearts, sliced
¹/4 cup chopped sundried tomatoes
¹/2 cup grated mozzarella cheese

olive oil to brush
¹/4 cup freshly grated parmesan cheese

Dissolve the sugar in the warm water. Sprinkle the yeast over the water and set aside in a warm place for 10 minutes until frothy. Combine the flour and salt in a large bowl. Stir in the frothy yeast mixture and oil. Mix to a soft dough. Transfer the dough to a liberally floured surface and knead for 5 minutes until smooth and elastic. Place the dough in an oiled bowl. Turn the dough to coat with oil. Cover with plastic wrap and stand in a warm place for 45 minutes until the dough is well risen. Divide the dough into 4 equal portions. Roll each portion into a 20-cm-diameter circle. Cover half of each circle with filling ingredients to within 1 cm of the edge of the dough — first, spread with the tapenade, then with layers of feta, capsicums, artichokes, sundried tomatoes and mozzarella. Lightly brush the edge of the dough with water. Fold the unfilled portion of dough over the filling and crimp edges together to seal. Transfer the calzone to a lightly greased baking tray. Brush lightly with oil. Sprinkle with parmesan. Bake at 220°C for 10 minutes, then reduce the temperature to 200°C and bake for a further 10–15 minutes until golden. *Makes 4.*

# HAM AND VEGETABLE FRITTATA

2 tablespoons oil
1 onion, finely chopped
1 cup small broccoli florets
2 cloves garlic, crushed
1 tablespoon Dijon mustard
8 eggs

salt and freshly ground black
   pepper to season
2 cups diced cooked potatoes
   (about 2 large potatoes)
4 slices ham, diced
1½ cups grated cheddar cheese

Heat oil in a heavy-based 25 cm frying pan with a heatproof handle. Cook onion, broccoli, garlic and mustard over a medium heat for 5 minutes. Lightly beat eggs and salt and pepper. Add potatoes and ham to pan, stirring to combine. Spread mixture evenly over base of pan. Reduce heat to low. Pour eggs evenly over vegetable mixture. Sprinkle with cheese. Cook for about 8 minutes until frittata is half cooked. Meanwhile, preheat oven grill. Place frittata under grill for 3–4 minutes until set and golden. Leave in pan for 5 minutes before cutting into wedges. Serve warm or cold. *Serves 4.*

# KUMARA SOUP

25 g butter
1 large kumara, peeled and chopped
1 onion, chopped
1 large potato, chopped
1½ teaspoons hot curry powder

3 cups chicken stock
1 cup milk
salt and freshly ground black pepper
chives to garnish

Melt butter in a saucepan. Add kumara, onion, potato and curry powder. Cook for 5 minutes until onion is soft. Stir in stock and bring to the boil. Simmer gently until vegetables are tender. Purée in a food processor or blender until smooth. Stir in milk. Reheat until almost boiling. Season to taste with salt and pepper. Ladle into warm bowls. Garnish with chives. *Serves 6–8.*

# LAMB SATAY

4 lean lamb leg steaks
1 tablespoon chopped coriander
2 teaspoons oil
1 teaspoon sambal oelek or chilli paste
bamboo skewers soaked in
   cold water for 30 minutes

SAUCE

¼ cup soy sauce
¼ cup chopped spring onions
1 teaspoon sambal oelek or chilli paste
2 tablespoons lemon or lime juice

Trim fat from meat, cut it into small cubes and put in a bowl. Add coriander, oil and sambal oelek. Leave to marinate for 30 minutes. Thread meat onto soaked bamboo skewers. Grill for 10 minutes or until just cooked, turning occasionally. Serve with sauce. To make the sauce, combine all ingredients. **Serves 4.** *(Below left)*

# LEEK AND POTATO SOUP

5 medium potatoes, peeled and chopped
2 teaspoons oil or butter
2 small leeks, thinly sliced
1 clove garlic, crushed
200 g bacon pieces, finely chopped
6 cups chicken stock

1 bay leaf
2 sprigs parsley
1 cup milk
¼ cup chopped parsley
salt and freshly ground black pepper

Cook potatoes in boiling water until tender. Drain and mash. Set aside. Heat oil in a large saucepan. Add leeks, garlic and bacon. Cook without colouring until leeks are tender. Pour in stock. Add bay leaf and parsley sprigs. Bring to the boil. Reduce heat and simmer for 20 minutes. Remove bay leaf and parsley sprigs. Add mashed potato. Simmer for 15 minutes. Stir in milk and parsley. Season to taste with salt and pepper. Ladle into warm bowls. Garnish with a sprinkle of pepper. **Serves 6-8.** *(Top left)*

# MARINATED PORK SPARE RIBS

½ cup tomato sauce
½ cup soy sauce
½ cup plum sauce
1 tablespoon sweet chilli sauce
   (or more to taste)

1 teaspoon crushed garlic
1.5 kg pork spare ribs

Combine the four sauces and garlic. Mix well. Using a sharp knife, divide spare ribs into 1 or 2 bone sections. Place ribs in a single layer over the base of a roasting dish. Pour over marinade. Toss ribs until evenly coated. Cover with plastic wrap and refrigerate for at least 1 hour or up to 8 hours. Bake at 200°C for 12–15 minutes, turning regularly, until cooked through. Turn oven to grill and cook ribs for a further 5 minutes, turning 2 or 3 times, until lightly browned. **Serves 4.** *(Middle right)*

# MEXICAN QUESADILLAS

2 cups shredded cooked chicken
1½ cups grated tasty cheddar cheese
½ cup bottled tomato salsa

4 gherkins, sliced (optional)
8 x 20-cm-diameter flour tortillas

Combine chicken, cheese, salsa and gherkins in a bowl. Mix well. Lay 4 of the tortillas on a flat surface. Divide mixture between the tortillas, spreading to within 1 cm of the edge. Sandwich with remaining tortillas, pressing lightly to consolidate. Heat a large frying pan. Using a large fish slice, transfer 1 tortilla to the pan. Cook over a medium heat for 2 minutes. Carefully turn and cook for a further 2 minutes or until cheese has melted. Remove from pan. Repeat with remaining tortillas. To serve, cut into wedges. **Serves 4 as a snack.** *(Below left)*

# MINI MEAT PIES

2 teaspoons oil
500 g lean beef mince
½ cup tomato sauce
2 tablespoons tomato paste
¾ cup water

salt and freshly ground black
pepper to season
6 sheets ready-rolled frozen flaky puff
pastry, thawed
milk to seal and glaze

Heat oil in a frying pan. Cook mince for 4–5 minutes until browned. Stir in tomato sauce, tomato paste and water. Simmer over a low heat for 15 minutes, or until most of the liquid has been absorbed. Season to taste. Remove from heat. Cool. Using an 8-cm-diameter biscuit cutter, stamp 20 rounds from pastry sheets. Press into deep-pan muffin tins. Spoon cold mixture into pastry cases. Brush edge of pastry lightly with milk. Using a 7-cm-diameter biscuit cutter, stamp 20 tops from remaining pastry. Place over pies, pressing lightly around the edge to seal. Brush tops lightly with milk. Bake at 200°C for 16–18 minutes until golden. Cool in tins for 2–3 minutes before removing. Serve hot. **Makes 20.** *(Above right)*

# POTATO, CAULIFLOWER AND CHICKPEA CURRY

2 tablespoons oil
1 onion, chopped
2 cloves garlic, crushed
2 teaspoons grated root ginger
1 teaspoon ground cumin
1 teaspoon ground coriander
½ teaspoon chilli powder
2 whole cloves
pinch of fenugreek

5 medium potatoes, peeled and diced
400 ml can coconut cream (or 400 g can
     tomatoes in juice + 1 tablespoon sugar)
1 small cauliflower, cut into florets
300 g can chickpeas, drained
juice of 1 lemon
¼ cup chopped coriander
chopped coriander to garnish
cooked basmati rice to serve

Heat oil in a heavy-based saucepan. Cook onion for 5 minutes until soft. Add garlic, ginger and spices. Cook for 2–3 minutes, stirring constantly. Add potatoes and cook, stirring constantly, for 2–3 minutes. Add coconut cream. Simmer for about 20 minutes, until potato is tender. Add cauliflower and chickpeas. Cook for about 10 minutes until cauliflower is tender. Just before serving, stir in lemon juice and coriander. Garnish with chopped coriander. Serve with rice. *Serves 4.*

# PUMPKIN AND CHICKEN FILO PIES

2 cups (275 g) peeled, seeded
   and diced pumpkin
1 large potato, peeled and diced
1 tablespoon butter to mash
2 tablespoons oil
2 onions, finely chopped
2 teaspoons ground cumin
1 teaspoon garam masala

1 single boneless, skinless
   chicken breast, diced
1 teaspoon crushed garlic
1 cup grated tasty cheddar cheese
salt and freshly ground black
   pepper to season
50 g butter, melted
18 sheets filo pastry

Cook the pumpkin and potato in boiling water until tender. Drain. Add the butter and mash. Heat the oil in a frying pan and cook onion, cumin, garam masala and chicken for 6–8 minutes until onion is soft. Add the garlic and cook for 2 minutes. Combine mashed vegetable mixture, chicken mixture and cheese. Season. Brush 12 deep-pan muffin tins with melted butter. For each pie, lightly brush a sheet of filo pastry with melted butter. Fold in half widthways, then brush with butter. Fold in half again. Line prepared tins with the pastry. Spoon the filling into pastry shells. Cut the remaining 6 sheets of filo pastry in half widthways. Scrunch each portion into a ball and place on top of pies. Brush with melted butter. Bake at 190°C for 20 minutes until golden. Stand for 8–10 minutes before serving. ***Makes 12.*** *(Below left)*

# SPINACH AND FETA FILO PARCELS

250 g frozen spinach, thawed
250 g cottage cheese
100 g feta cheese, crumbled
1/3 cup toasted pinenuts
1 egg
2 cloves garlic, crushed

pinch of nutmeg
salt and freshly ground black
   pepper to season
16 sheets filo pastry
50 g butter, melted

Squeeze spinach dry. Combine spinach, cottage and feta cheeses, pinenuts, egg, garlic and nutmeg in a bowl. Mix well. Season with salt and pepper. To make each parcel, place a sheet of filo pastry on a flat surface. Brush with melted butter. Top with another sheet of filo, brush again with melted butter, then fold in half to make a rectangle. Spoon spinach mixture along one narrow end of the pastry. Fold edges in and roll up to encase filling. Place parcels on an oven tray brushed with butter. Brush parcels with remaining butter. Bake at 190°C for 12–15 minutes until golden. ***Makes 8.*** *(Above right)*

# SUMMER CALZONE

| DOUGH | FILLING |
|---|---|

**DOUGH**

1½ teaspoons sugar
300 ml warm water
2 tablespoons Edmonds active yeast
3 cups Champion high grade flour
1½ teaspoons salt
¼ cup olive oil

**FILLING**

2 tablespoons Pesto (see page 182)
1½ cups grated mozzarella cheese
2 large tomatoes, sliced
1 red capsicum, roasted (see page 188
    for method), sliced
40 g thinly sliced salami

freshly ground black pepper
olive oil to brush
rock salt or grated parmesan
    cheese to sprinkle

Dissolve sugar in the warm water. Sprinkle yeast over water and set aside in a warm place for 10 minutes until frothy. Combine flour and salt in a large bowl. Stir in frothy yeast mixture and oil. Mix to a soft dough. Transfer dough to a liberally floured surface and knead for 5 minutes until smooth and elastic. Place dough in an oiled bowl. Turn dough to coat with oil. Cover with plastic wrap and stand in a warm place for 45 minutes until dough is well risen. Divide dough in half. Roll each portion into a 25-cm-diameter circle. Place one circle on a lightly greased baking tray. Spread with pesto to within 1 cm of the dough edge. Sprinkle mozzarella cheese over the pesto, then top with tomato, red capsicum and salami. Season with pepper. Brush edge of dough with a little oil. Position the remaining circle of dough on top and seal edges with your fingertips. Brush top lightly with a little olive oil. Sprinkle with rock salt or parmesan cheese. Bake at 220°C for 10 minutes, then reduce temperature to 200°C and bake for a further 15–20 minutes until golden. Serve in wedges. *Serves 6.*

# SUPER SANDWICHES

With such an extensive range of superb breads baked daily in supermarkets, bakeries and even at home, the humble sandwich takes on a new lease of life. The possibilities for delicious, nutritious sandwiches as snacks, or even main meals, are endless.

### TABOULEH STUFFED PITA BREAD

Fill *pita bread* with *Tabouleh* (see recipe below) and *shredded cooked chicken* or *smoked (or roast) beef.* *(Top left)*

### BRIE, BACON AND ONION MARMALADE SANDWICHES

Grill *bacon rashers* until lightly crisp. Top *lightly buttered bread* with warm bacon, *sliced brie cheese, sliced avocado* and *Onion Marmalade* (see recipe below).

### SMOKED CHICKEN AND ASPARAGUS ROLLS

Fill *bread rolls* with *blanched asparagus spears, shredded smoked chicken, sliced tomato* and *lettuce.* Garnish with a dollop of *mayonnaise.*

### TUNA AND AVOCADO SANDWICHES

Drain *tinned tuna in brine* and combine with *finely chopped spring onions* and sufficient *mayonnaise* to moisten. Season with *freshly ground black pepper.* Top *lightly buttered bread* with *lettuce,* the tuna mixture and *sliced avocado.* *(Middle)*

### HAM AND CHEESE WRAPS

Top a slice of *lightly buttered bread* with *lettuce.* Place *sliced ham* and *thinly sliced cheese* on one half of the lettuce. Garnish with a little *pickle.* Fold bread over to encase the filling. Secure with a toothpick. The bread must be fresh to fold successfully.

# TABOULEH

1 cup burghul (cracked wheat)
2 tablespoons fresh mint, chopped
1 cup parsley, chopped
2 tomatoes, chopped

2 tablespoons oil
¼ cup lemon juice
salt and freshly ground black
　　pepper to season

Put burghul in a bowl. Cover with boiling water. Leave to stand for 30 minutes. Stir and drain if necessary. Add the mint, parsley, tomatoes, oil and lemon juice. Stir to combine. Season to taste with salt and pepper. Chill before serving. *Serves 6.* *(Below left)*

# ONION MARMALADE

¼ cup olive oil
4 onions, sliced
2 tablespoons brown sugar
2 cloves garlic, crushed

¼ cup dry white wine
salt and freshly ground black
　　pepper to season

Heat oil in a frying pan. Cook onions over a very low heat, stirring occasionally, for 30 minutes. Add brown sugar and garlic and cook for 2 minutes, stirring constantly. Add wine and cook for a further 8–10 minutes. Season to taste with salt and pepper. Cool. Store in a covered container in the refrigerator. This Onion Marmalade will keep for 1 week. *(Below right)*

# TOSTADAS

8 x 20-cm-diameter flour tortillas
450 g can refried beans
3 tablespoons bottled tomato salsa
2 small avocados, sliced
2 cups shredded lettuce
2 cups sliced cooked chicken meat
16 cherry tomatoes, halved
250 g sour cream, to serve

### DRESSING
2 tablespoons lemon or lime juice
1/4 teaspoon salt
1/2 teaspoon ground cumin
1/4 cup oil

Warm tortillas according to instructions on the packet. Heat refried beans and tomato salsa in a saucepan. Spread each tortilla with bean mixture. Top with avocado slices, lettuce, chicken and tomatoes. Serve with sour cream. Sprinkle with dressing. To make the dressing, combine all ingredients. Mix well. *Serves 4.* (Below)

# TURKISH LAMB PATTIES WITH YOGHURT SAUCE AND PITA BREAD

### LAMB PATTIES
500 g lean lamb mince
2 teaspoons crushed garlic
1 teaspoon ground cumin
1/2 teaspoon allspice
2 tablespoons chopped oregano
   (or 2 teaspoons dried oregano)
1/4 cup chopped parsley
salt and freshly ground black
   pepper to season
oil to brush

### YOGHURT SAUCE
1 cup natural unsweetened yoghurt
1 clove garlic, crushed
freshly ground black pepper

pita bread, shredded lettuce, sliced
   tomato, sliced cucumber, to serve

To make the patties, combine all ingredients in a bowl. Mix well. Brush the base of a roasting dish with oil. Take teaspoonsful of patty mixture and roll into balls. Place in roasting dish. Flatten patties slightly with the palm of your hand. Brush top of patties with oil. Preheat oven grill. Grill patties, 10 cm from the heat source, for about 8 minutes, turning once during cooking. While patties are cooking, prepare the yoghurt sauce. Combine all ingredients in a bowl. To serve, tear pita breads in half. Fill with salad ingredients and patties. Drizzle with yoghurt sauce. Serve immediately. *Serves 4.* (Top)

# SALADS

# CHICKEN AND ASPARAGUS SALAD WITH MUSTARD DRESSING

### DRESSING
*2 tablespoons olive oil*
*2 tablespoons freshly squeezed*
*orange juice*
*1 tablespoon chopped parsley*
*2 teaspoons wholegrain mustard*
*salt and freshly ground black*
*pepper to season*

### SALAD
*20 asparagus spears*
*100 g snowpeas*
*2 cups sliced cooked chicken meat*
*2 firm, ripe avocados, peeled and sliced*
*½ cup quality walnut pieces*

To make the dressing, combine all ingredients. Mix well. To make the salad, snap woody ends off asparagus. Cook in a little boiling water for 3–4 minutes until just tender. Drain and cool under cold running water. Add snowpeas to boiling water. Bring back to the boil, then tip into a sieve. Cool under cold running water. Drain well. Combine salad ingredients in a bowl. Pour over dressing and toss gently. Serve with fresh bread. **Serves 4.** *(Below left)*

# GRILLED CHICKEN CAESAR SALAD

*4 single boneless skinless chicken breasts*
*¼ cup olive oil*
*2 tablespoons lemon juice*
*freshly ground black pepper to season*
*2 cups stale bread cubes (French bread*
*or toast sliced bread is ideal)*

*1 cos lettuce*
*12 anchovy fillets*
*shavings of parmesan cheese*
*Caesar Salad Dressing (see page 181)*

Place chicken breasts between 2 sheets of plastic wrap. Beat lightly with a heavy object (e.g. a rolling pin) to flatten to an even thickness of about 1 cm. Place in a single layer in a shallow dish. Combine 2 tablespoons of the oil, lemon juice and pepper. Pour over chicken, turning to coat. Cover and refrigerate for 2–4 hours. Cook chicken under a preheated grill or on a barbecue for 4–5 minutes on each side until cooked through. Set aside to cool. To make the croutons, pour remaining oil into a frying pan. Heat pan. Add bread cubes and cook until golden, turning frequently. Wash and dry lettuce leaves. Slice chicken into strips. Combine lettuce, chicken, anchovy fillets and parmesan cheese in a bowl. Pour over dressing. Toss to combine. Scatter over croutons. **Serves 4.** *(Above right)*

# LUNCHBOX PASTA SALAD

150 g dried pasta bows
12 cherry tomatoes, halved
   (or 4 tomatoes, quartered)
1 green capsicum, seeded,
   cored and diced
100 g cheddar cheese, cut in small dice
½ cup toasted pinenuts (optional)

### DRESSING

2 tablespoons olive oil
2 tablespoons white wine vinegar
2 tablespoons freshly squeezed
   orange juice
1 tablespoon chopped parsley
salt and freshly ground black
   pepper to season

Cook pasta according to packet instructions. Transfer to a sieve. Cool under cold running water, then drain thoroughly. Combine all salad ingredients in a large bowl. Pour over dressing and toss to combine. To make the dressing, place all ingredients in a jar. Secure the lid and shake vigorously. To include this salad in the lunchbox, transfer to a lidded container. Include a fork. **Serves 4.** *(Below left)*

# ORZO PASTA SALAD

### DRESSING

¼ cup olive oil
2 tablespoons DYC white wine vinegar
2 tablespoons freshly squeezed
   orange juice
1 tablespoon chopped basil
2 cloves garlic, crushed
salt and freshly ground black
   pepper to season

### SALAD

300 g orzo pasta
50 g sliced salami, diced
½ cup pistachio nuts
¼ cup chopped sundried tomatoes
15 stuffed green olives, halved

To make the dressing, combine all ingredients. Mix well. For the salad, cook the pasta in boiling water for 10 minutes until al dente. Tip into a sieve, then rinse under cold running water. Drain thoroughly. Combine all salad ingredients in a bowl. Pour dressing over and toss lightly to combine. **Serves 4.** *(Above right)*

# SALMON AND PASTA NIÇOISE SALAD

### DRESSING
¼ cup olive oil
¼ cup lemon juice
2 tablespoons chopped parsley
1 tablespoon wholegrain mustard
freshly ground black pepper to season

### SALAD
250 g Diamond Small Seashells
200 g green beans
12 cherry tomatoes, halved
210 g can salmon, drained
   and roughly flaked
4 hard-boiled eggs, shelled and quartered
16–20 pitted black olives (preferably
   Kalamata olives)

To make the dressing, combine all ingredients. Mix well. For the salad, cook pasta according to instructions on the packet. Tip into a sieve and refresh under cold running water. Drain thoroughly. Trim ends from beans. Plunge beans into boiling water. Allow to return to the boil, then cook for 1 minute or until just tender. Tip into a sieve and refresh under cold running water. Drain. Combine all salad ingredients in a bowl. Pour dressing over salad and toss lightly to combine. *Serves 4.*

# SMOKED CHICKEN, PAWPAW AND MACADAMIA NUT SALAD

### DRESSING

*½ pawpaw*
*1 tablespoon lemon or lime juice*
*1 tablespoon olive oil*
*¼ cup loosely packed coriander leaves*
*freshly ground black pepper to season*

### SALAD

*½ pawpaw*
*2 cups shredded smoked chicken*
*4 handfuls mixed salad greens,*
*    washed and dried*
*2 spring onions, sliced*
*½ cup salted macadamia nuts,*
*    roughly chopped*

To make the dressing, cut pawpaw in half and remove seeds. Reserve half for the salad. Peel and roughly chop remaining half. Place in a food processor with remaining dressing ingredients. Blend until smooth. For the salad, cut pawpaw half into narrow slices, then peel. Cut slices into 3–4 cm lengths. Place chicken in a bowl. Pour half the dressing over the chicken and toss to coat. Place remaining dressing in a small jug to accompany the salad. To serve, place a handful of salad greens on 4 serving plates. Top with chicken, pawpaw, spring onions and nuts. Serve with fresh crusty bread, accompanied by jug of dressing. *Serves 2–3 as a light meal.*
*(Top right)*

# SPINACH, FETA AND BACON SALAD

### DRESSING

*¼ cup olive oil*
*2 tablespoons balsamic vinegar*
*1 tablespoon lemon juice*
*1 teaspoon brown sugar*
*salt and freshly ground black*
*    pepper to season*

### SALAD

*3 slices toast-cut bread*
*2 tablespoons olive oil*
*8 rashers rindless bacon,*
*    roughly chopped*
*150 g baby spinach leaves,*
*    washed and dried*
*200 g feta cheese, diced*
*¼ cup toasted pinenuts (optional)*

To make the dressing, combine all ingredients. Mix well. For the salad, cut bread into small cubes. Heat oil in a frying pan. Toss bread over a medium heat until golden. Remove from pan. Add bacon and cook for 5–6 minutes until beginning to crisp. Remove from pan. Cool. Place all salad ingredients in a bowl. Pour over dressing and toss lightly to combine. *Serves 4.*
*(Top left and below)*

# THAI-STYLE BEEF SALAD

### DRESSING

¼ cup soy sauce
¼ cup fish sauce
1 tablespoon oil
2 tablespoons lime or lemon juice
2 tablespoons chopped mint
2 tablespoons chopped coriander
2 cloves garlic, crushed
1 small red chilli, seeded
   and finely chopped

### SALAD

750 g piece eye fillet steak
salt and freshly ground black pepper
2 courgettes
2 carrots
150 g green beans, trimmed and halved
1 red capsicum, seeded and thinly sliced
1 yellow capsicum, seeded
   and thinly sliced
12–16 cherry tomatoes, halved
   (or 4 regular tomatoes, quartered)

To make the dressing, combine all ingredients. Mix well. Preheat oven to 220°C. Season beef all over with a little salt and pepper. Heat oil in a heavy-based frying pan until pan is very hot. Cook beef for 3–4 minutes, turning regularly, until meat is seared all over. Transfer to a roasting dish. Bake for 10–12 minutes. The meat should be medium-rare. Set aside to cool. Meanwhile, prepare the vegetables. Trim ends off courgettes and carrots. Peel carrots. Using a vegetable peeler, peel long strips from the courgettes and carrots. Plunge into boiling water for 10 seconds to blanch. Tip into a sieve and refresh under cold running water. Blanch beans in the same way for 30 seconds. Tip into a sieve and refresh under cold running water. Slice beef thinly. Place all salad ingredients in a bowl. Pour over dressing and toss to combine. *Serves 4–6. (Below)*

# TUNA PASTA SALAD

### DRESSING

¾ cup mayonnaise
2 tablespoons lemon juice
1 tablespoon DYC white wine vinegar
1 teaspoon wholegrain mustard
2 tablespoons chopped parsley
salt and freshly ground black
   pepper to season

### SALAD

500 g Diamond Italian Style
   Frilled Shells
2 red onions, diced
4 gherkins, diced
1 red capsicum, seeded and diced
2 carrots, peeled and cut into
   matchsticks
8 cherry tomatoes, halved
   (or 2 regular tomatoes, quartered)
185 g can tuna in brine, drained

To make the dressing, combine all ingredients. Mix well. For the salad, cook pasta according to the instructions on the packet. Drain in a sieve and cool under cold running water. Drain thoroughly. Combine all salad ingredients in a bowl. Pour over dressing and toss lightly to combine. *Serves 4. (Top left)*

# WARM MEDITERRANEAN LAMB SALAD

1 small eggplant
2 courgettes
about ¼ cup olive oil
1 red capsicum, roasted
   (see page 188 for method)
1 yellow capsicum, roasted
   (see page 188 for method)
250 g lamb fillets
salt and freshly ground black pepper
1 red onion, thinly sliced
5–6 canned artichoke hearts,
   halved (optional)

### DRESSING

3 tablespoons olive oil
1 teaspoon finely grated orange zest
2 tablespoons freshly squeezed
   orange juice
1 teaspoon liquid honey
2 tablespoons chopped basil
salt and freshly ground black
   pepper to season

Trim ends off eggplant and courgettes. Cut vegetables lengthwise into 5-mm-thick strips. Preheat oven grill. Brush vegetables all over with olive oil. Place in a single layer on a baking tray. Grill for 4–5 minutes, turning occasionally, until vegetables are cooked through and golden. Cut capsicums into 1-cm-wide strips. Season lamb fillets with salt and pepper. Heat a little oil in a heavy-based frying pan. Cook lamb for 8–10 minutes, turning occasionally. The lamb should be slightly pink on inside. Set aside for 4–5 minutes before slicing. To make the dressing, combine all ingredients in a bowl. Mix well. Combine all salad ingredients in a bowl. Pour over dressing. Toss lightly to combine. Serve salad immediately, accompanied by fresh bread. *Serves 4.*

# WILD RICE SALAD

1¹/₂ cups wild rice
¹/₂ cup toasted pistachio nuts
3 spring onions, chopped
1 red capsicum, cored, seeded and diced
¹/₄ cup chopped sundried tomatoes
100 g diced feta cheese, or 4 rashers
   rindless bacon, diced and
   cooked until crisp

### DRESSING

2 tablespoons olive oil
2 tablespoons freshly squeezed
   orange juice
2 tablespoons chopped fresh herbs,
   e.g. parsley or coriander
1 teaspoon wholegrain mustard

Cook rice according to instructions on packet. Tip into a sieve and rinse under cold running water. Drain thoroughly. Combine all salad ingredients in a bowl. To make the dressing, combine all ingredients. Mix well. Pour dressing over salad and toss. *Serves 4.*

# MAIN MEALS

# BEEF, CASHEW NUT AND VEGETABLE STIR-FRY IN BLACK BEAN SAUCE

*750 g lean, fast-fry steak, e.g. rump,*
*  fillet or porterhouse*
*3 tablespoons soy sauce*
*2 tablespoons dry sherry*
*2 tablespoons oil (preferably sesame oil)*
*1 onion, thinly sliced*
*2 carrots, peeled and thinly sliced*
*227 g can bamboo shoots, drained*

*¼ cup black bean sauce*
*½ cup water*
*2 teaspoons Edmonds Fielder's cornflour*
*  mixed to a paste with*
*  1 tablespoon water*
*1 cup mung bean sprouts*
*1 cup toasted cashew nuts*
*cooked rice or noodles to serve*

Cut meat into 5-mm-wide strips. Combine meat, soy sauce and sherry in a bowl. Stand for 20 minutes. Heat 1 tablespoon of the oil in a wok or heavy-based frying pan. Stir-fry onion and carrot for 4–5 minutes until soft. Remove from pan. Add remaining oil to pan. Stir-fry meat for 2–3 minutes over a high heat until just cooked through. Return onion and carrot to pan. Add bamboo shoots, black bean sauce and water. Stir well. Add cornflour paste and stir continuously until sauce thickens and comes to the boil. Add bean sprouts and nuts. Toss to combine. Serve immediately on a bed of cooked noodles or rice. **Serves 4.** *(Top right)*

# BEEF FAJITAS

*500 g lean, fast-fry steak, e.g. rump,*
*  fillet or porterhouse*
*2 teaspoons paprika*
*1 tablespoon ground cumin*
*½ teaspoon chilli powder*
*1 teaspoon dried oregano*
*¼ teaspoon salt*
*1 clove garlic, crushed*

*1 tablespoon lemon juice*
*2 tablespoons oil*
*1 large onion, sliced*
*1 red capsicum, seeded and thinly sliced*
*1 green or yellow capsicum,*
*  seeded and thinly sliced*
*flour tortillas, Guacamole (see page 52)*
*  and sour cream to serve*

Thinly slice meat and place in a bowl. Combine paprika, cumin, chilli powder, oregano, salt and garlic. Sprinkle over meat and toss to combine. Add lemon juice and toss. Heat 1 tablespoon of oil in a heavy-based frying pan. Cook onion and capsicums over a high heat for 5 minutes until soft. Remove from pan and keep warm. Add remaining oil to pan. Add meat and cook over a high heat for 6–8 minutes until browned. Return vegetables to pan and toss to heat through. Serve immediately with flour tortillas, guacamole and sour cream. **Serves 3–4.** *(Below right)*

N.B. The quantities of paprika and chilli powder used in the above recipe produce a medium-spiced dish. For a milder flavour, use *1 teaspoon paprika* and *¼ teaspoon chilli powder*. For a spicier flavour, use *3 teaspoons paprika* and *1 teaspoon chilli powder*.

# CHARGRILLED VEGETABLE LASAGNE

### TOMATO SAUCE
*1 tablespoon oil*
*1 onion, finely chopped*
*2 x 400 g cans tomatoes in juice*
*1 teaspoon crushed garlic*
*salt and freshly ground black*
*    pepper to season*

*1 medium eggplant*
*4 courgettes*
*2 capsicums, any colour*
*about ⅓ cup olive oil to brush*

*150 g Diamond Italian Style*
*    Wide Lasagne*
*1½ cups grated tasty cheddar cheese*

To make the tomato sauce, heat oil in a frying pan. Cook onion for 5 minutes until soft. Add tomatoes, garlic and seasonings. Break up tomatoes with a wooden spoon. Simmer for about 25 minutes until sauce is thick. While the sauce is cooking, prepare vegetables. Trim ends off eggplant and courgettes. Cut eggplant into 5-mm-thick round slices and courgettes lengthwise into 5-mm-thick slices. Halve capsicums. Core and seed, then cut into 2.5-cm-wide strips. Brush vegetables all over with olive oil. Place eggplant slices in a single layer in a baking dish. Place under a preheated grill, turning regularly until vegetables begin to brown. Repeat this cooking process with the courgettes and capsicums. Cook lasagne in boiling water for about 10 minutes, until al dente. Drain. Lay half the lasagne over the base of a 20 x 24 cm rectangular ovenproof dish. Top with half the grilled vegetables, then half the tomato sauce. Repeat these layers, finishing with the sauce. Sprinkle with cheese. Bake at 180°C for 25–30 minutes. Stand for 5 minutes. Serve with a tossed salad and crusty bread. *Serves 3.*

# CHEESY SESAME-COATED CHICKEN

8 chicken drumsticks
2 tablespoons Champion standard
   grade flour
2 tablespoons grated parmesan cheese
1 teaspoon chicken stock powder

¼ teaspoon mixed herbs
2 tablespoons dry breadcrumbs
2 teaspoons sesame seeds
oil

Remove skin from chicken. Moisten chicken slightly with water. Combine flour, parmesan cheese, stock powder, herbs, breadcrumbs and sesame seeds. Put this mixture into a plastic bag. Add 2 drumsticks to bag and shake to coat. Repeat with remaining chicken, coating only 2 at a time. Place drumsticks in a lightly oiled baking dish. Allow to stand for 15 minutes. Cook at 200°C for 25 minutes, or until juices run clear when tested. Turn chicken once or twice during the cooking time. Serve hot or cold. **Serves 4.** *(Below left)*

# CHICKEN CANNELLONI

1 tablespoon oil
1 onion, chopped
1 teaspoon crushed garlic
2 x 400 g cans tomatoes in juice
¼ cup tomato paste
salt and freshly ground black
   pepper to season

2 cups cooked finely diced chicken meat
½ cup cottage cheese
12 instant cannelloni tubes
1½ cups grated tasty cheddar cheese

Heat oil in a frying pan. Cook onion for 5 minutes until soft. Add garlic, tomatoes and tomato paste, breaking up tomatoes with a wooden spoon. Simmer for 25–30 minutes until sauce is thick. Season to taste with salt and pepper. Place chicken and cottage cheese in a bowl. Add 1 cup of the tomato sauce. Mix well. Fill cannelloni tubes with chicken mixture. Place in a single layer in a greased baking dish. Spread remaining tomato sauce evenly over the pasta. Sprinkle with cheese. Bake at 180°C for 25–30 minutes. Serve with a tossed salad. **Serves 4.** *(Above right)*

# CHICKEN AND AVOCADO RISOTTO

about 1.5 litres chicken stock
¼ cup olive oil
1 onion, finely sliced
2 cloves garlic, crushed
500 g arborio rice
1 cup dry white wine

2 cups cooked diced chicken
½ cup freshly grated parmesan cheese
1 firm, ripe avocado, peeled and diced
salt and freshly ground black
    pepper to season
2 tablespoons shredded basil leaves

Bring chicken stock to the boil in a saucepan. Heat oil in a heavy-based, deep-sided frying pan. Cook onion for 5 minutes until soft. Add garlic and rice and stir over a low heat for 2–3 minutes to toast the rice. Add wine and cook for 1 minute. Ladle over sufficient boiling stock to just cover the rice. Cook, stirring frequently and adding more stock to cover the rice as the liquid is absorbed. This will take about 18 minutes. Remove pan from the heat. Add chicken and parmesan to the pan. Stir to combine. Cover pan and stand for 3–4 minutes. Gently toss through avocado. Season. Pile onto warm serving plates. Garnish with shredded basil. **Serves 4.** *(Middle left)*

# CHICKEN CHOW MEIN

2 boneless, skinless chicken breasts
2 tablespoons soy sauce
2 teaspoons dry sherry
2 teaspoons Edmonds Fielder's cornflour
½ teaspoon grated root ginger
2 tablespoons oil
1 onion, quartered
2 cloves garlic, crushed

1 cup broccoli florets
½ cup sliced celery
1 red capsicum, seeded and sliced
½ cup chicken stock
2 teaspoons Edmonds Fielder's cornflour
¼ teaspoon freshly ground black pepper
1 tablespoon soy sauce
crispy noodles to serve

Cut chicken into strips. Combine chicken, first measure of soy sauce, sherry, first measure of cornflour and root ginger. Set aside to marinate for 30 minutes. Heat oil in a wok or large heavy-based frying pan. Add onion and garlic and cook for 5 minutes until onion is clear. Add chicken and quickly stir-fry until meat is browned all over. Add broccoli, celery and capsicum. Stir-fry until vegetables are bright in colour. In a bowl combine stock, second measure of cornflour and pepper. Add to wok, stirring until mixture thickens and comes to the boil. Sprinkle with second measure of soy sauce. Toss. Serve with crispy noodles. **Serves 4.** *(Below right)*

# CHICKEN CURRY

2 tablespoons oil
1 onion, chopped
2 cloves garlic, crushed
2 teaspoons grated root ginger
2 medium potatoes, peeled and diced
2 stalks celery, sliced

4 skinless, boneless chicken breasts, diced
2 tablespoons curry powder
2 tablespoons Champion standard
    grade flour
1½ cups chicken stock
½ cup cream

Heat oil in a large saucepan. Add onion, garlic, ginger, potato and celery. Cook for 5 minutes, stirring frequently. Add chicken and cook for 3–4 minutes, stirring constantly. Stir in curry powder and flour and cook for 30 seconds. Add stock. Cover pan and bring to the boil. Reduce heat and simmer for 25 minutes, stirring occasionally, until chicken is tender. Stir in cream. Serve with cooked rice. **Serves 4.** *(Top right)*

# CHILLI CON CARNE

1 tablespoon oil
2 onions, chopped
1 clove garlic, crushed
1 green capsicum, chopped
500 g lean beef mince
1½ teaspoons chilli powder

1 cup water
290 g can tomato paste
¼ teaspoon oregano
425 g can red kidney beans, drained
cooked rice to serve
chives for garnish

Heat oil in a large frying pan. Add onions, garlic and capsicum. Cook for 5 minutes until onion and capsicum are soft. Stir in meat and cook until meat is browned. Add chilli powder, water, tomato paste and oregano. Bring to the boil, stirring constantly. Reduce heat and simmer gently for 30 minutes or until mixture is thick. Add kidney beans to pan. Cook for a further 3–4 minutes, stirring frequently. Serve on a bed of rice or with rice moulds. To make rice moulds, press cooked rice firmly into oiled teacups. Invert cup onto serving plate and tap gently to release the moulded rice. Garnish with snipped chives. *Serves 4.* *(Below left)*

# GRILLED FISH WITH PARMESAN CRUST

½ cup fresh breadcrumbs
   (white or brown)
½ cup freshly grated parmesan cheese
1 tablespoon wholegrain mustard
2 tablespoons melted butter
1 teaspoon finely grated lemon zest

salt and freshly ground black
   pepper to season
4 fillets boneless white fish,
   e.g. gurnard, tarakihi, snapper
lemon wedges to garnish

To make the crumb topping, combine breadcrumbs, cheese, mustard, melted butter, lemon zest and salt and pepper. Mix well. Preheat grill. Pat fish fillets dry with paper towels. Place on a greased baking tray. Divide crumb mixture between fish fillets, spreading evenly to cover. Grill for about 8–10 minutes (cooking time will depend on the thickness of the fish). The fish is cooked when the flesh turns white. Garnish with lemon wedges. Serve with a tossed salad and fresh bread. *Serves 4.* *(Above right)*

# HAMBURGERS

500 g lean beef mince
1 onion, finely chopped
1 clove garlic, crushed
2 tablespoons tomato sauce
2 tablespoons chopped herbs,
   e.g. parsley, oregano
⅓ cup Fleming's rolled oats
1 egg

salt and freshly ground black
   pepper to season
a little oil to cook
4 hamburger buns
salad ingredients of your choice,
   e.g. lettuce leaves, sliced cheese,
   sliced tomato, sliced avocado,
   sliced cucumber

To make the hamburger patties, combine mince, onion, garlic, tomato sauce, herbs, rolled oats, egg, salt and pepper in a bowl. Mix well. Divide mixture into 4 equal portions. Shape into patties about 9 cm in diameter. Place patties in a single layer on a plate and cover with plastic wrap. Refrigerate for 30 minutes. Pour sufficient oil into a heavy-based frying pan to just cover the base. Cook patties over a medium heat for about 7 minutes on each side, until golden and cooked through. While the patties are cooking, prepare hamburger buns. Cut buns in half horizontally. Place cut-side up on a baking tray. Place under a preheated grill to toast lightly. Layer salad ingredients of your choice and a patty on the bottom half of each bun. Top with other half of bun. Serve immediately. **Makes 4.**

# LAMB AND PRUNE TAGINE

1 cup pitted prunes
1 cup boiling water
2 tablespoons Champion standard
   grade flour
1 teaspoon ground cumin
1 teaspoon ground coriander
1 teaspoon cinnamon
salt and freshly ground black
   pepper to season

750 g lean diced lamb
1 tablespoon oil
2 onions, finely chopped
2 teaspoons Edmonds Fielder's cornflour
1 tablespoon water
¼ cup sliced almonds to garnish
coriander leaves to garnish

Place prunes in a bowl. Pour over water and allow to soak for 30 minutes. Combine flour, spices, salt and pepper in a bowl. Add lamb and toss until evenly coated. Transfer to a casserole dish. Heat oil in a frying pan. Cook onion for 5 minutes until soft. Transfer to casserole dish. Add prunes and water and stir well. Cover dish and bake at 180°C for 1–1½ hours until tender, adding a little more water if all the liquid is absorbed. Mix cornflour to a smooth paste with the water. Stir into meat, then cover and cook for a further 15 minutes. Garnish with almonds and coriander leaves. Serve with mashed potatoes and seasonal vegetables. *Serves 4.* *(Top right)*

# LAMB AND VEGETABLE STIR-FRY

500 g lean lamb leg steaks
2 tablespoons soy sauce
2 tablespoons dry sherry
1 tablespoon finely grated root ginger
3 tablespoons oil
1 onion, sliced
2 cloves garlic, crushed
3 stalks celery, sliced
1 carrot, peeled and thinly sliced

1 head broccoli, cut into small florets
¼ cup water
2 tablespoons soy sauce
2 tablespoons DYC malt vinegar
425 g can baby corn, drained
2 teaspoons Edmonds Fielder's cornflour
1 tablespoon water
cooked rice to serve

Remove any visible fat from the meat. Cut lamb into 1-cm-wide strips. Place in a bowl. Combine first measure of soy sauce, sherry and ginger. Pour over meat and stir. Set aside for 30 minutes. Heat 1 tablespoon of the oil in a wok or heavy-based frying pan. Stir-fry lamb over a high heat for 3–4 minutes until cooked through. Remove from pan. Heat remaining oil. Stir-fry onion, garlic, celery, carrot and broccoli for 4–5 minutes. Add first measure of water, soy sauce and vinegar. Cook for a further 3–4 minutes, stirring occasionally. Add corn and lamb. Cook for 2–3 minutes. Mix cornflour to a smooth paste with water. Add to wok, stirring until sauce thickens. Serve on a bed of rice. *Serves 4.* *(Below right)*

# LAMB CURRY

1½ tablespoons Champion standard
  grade flour
salt and freshly ground black pepper
750 g lean diced lamb
2 tablespoons oil
1 large onion, chopped
2 cloves garlic, crushed
1 tablespoon tomato paste

1½ teaspoons grated root ginger
1 teaspoon chopped fresh seeded chilli
1½ teaspoons ground cumin
1 teaspoon ground coriander
1 teaspoon ground cardamom
½ cup chicken stock
strips of red capsicum, to garnish
poppadoms, to serve

Combine flour, salt and pepper in a bowl. Coat meat in seasoned flour. Set aside. Heat oil in a large saucepan. Add onion and garlic and cook for 5 minutes until onion is clear. Remove with slotted spoon. Add half of the meat to pan and quickly brown all over. Remove from pan and repeat with remaining meat. Return meat and onion mixture to saucepan. Add tomato paste, ginger, chilli, cumin, coriander, cardamom and stock. Stir well. Bring to the boil. Cover, reduce heat and simmer gently for 1 hour or until meat is tender. Transfer to a warm serving dish. Garnish with strips of red capsicum. Serve with Cucumber and Mint Raita (see page 182) and poppadoms. **Serves 4.** *(Below left)*

# LANTERNA PASTA WITH ROASTED VEGETABLES AND PESTO

1 small eggplant
2 courgettes
2 red capsicums
1 yellow capsicum
2 tomatoes
1 teaspoon crushed garlic

¼ cup olive oil
375 g Diamond Italian Style
  Lanterna pasta
2 tablespoons Pesto (see page 182)
salt and freshly ground black pepper
freshly grated parmesan cheese, to serve

Trim ends off eggplant and courgettes. Halve capsicums and remove seeds. Cut all vegetables into 1.5-cm cubes. Spread vegetables in a single layer over the base of a roasting dish. Add garlic. Drizzle over oil and toss to coat. Bake at 230°C for 12–15 minutes, turning occasionally until vegetables are tender and the tomatoes mushy. While the vegetables are cooking, cook pasta according to packet instructions. Drain. Toss pesto and vegetables through pasta, ensuring all the juices from the roasting dish are scraped into the pasta. Season to taste with salt and pepper. Accompany with a bowl of freshly grated parmesan cheese. **Serves 4.** *(Above right)*

# MOROCCAN LAMB AND COUSCOUS PILAF

1 tablespoon Moroccan seasoning
300 g lamb fillets (about 5 fillets)
3 tablespoons olive oil
1 onion, finely chopped
½ cup freshly squeezed orange juice
    (2 oranges)
1 cup water
1 cup couscous

1 tablespoon butter
½ cup toasted slivered almonds
½ cup chopped dried apricots
¼ cup chopped mint
¼ cup chopped coriander
¼ cup chopped parsley
salt and freshly ground black
    pepper to season

Sprinkle seasoning over lamb fillets. Heat 2 tablespoons of the oil in a heavy-based frying pan. Cook lamb for 8–9 minutes until browned all over, turning occasionally. Remove fillets from pan and cover with foil to keep warm. Add remaining oil to pan and cook onion for 4–5 minutes until soft. Remove from pan and set aside. Place orange juice and water in a saucepan. Bring to the boil. Stir in couscous. Remove from heat, cover pan and stand for 2–3 minutes until the liquid has been absorbed. Add butter and place over a very low heat for 2 minutes, stirring constantly with a fork to separate the grains. Stir in cooked onion, almonds, apricots, mint, coriander and parsley. Season. Slice lamb thinly. Toss through couscous. *Serves 4.*

# MOUSSAKA

1 tablespoon salt
2 large eggplants, sliced
2 tablespoons olive oil
2 onions, chopped
2 cloves garlic, crushed
750 g lean lamb mince
400 g can tomatoes in juice,
   drained and chopped
290 g can tomato purée

½ cup chicken stock
salt and freshly ground black pepper
¼ cup oil
2 egg yolks
1 tablespoon Champion standard
   grade flour
250 g natural unsweetened yoghurt
¼ cup grated parmesan cheese

Sprinkle salt over eggplant and set aside for 30 minutes. Heat first measure of oil in a saucepan. Add onion and garlic and cook for 5 minutes until onion is soft. Add mince, stirring frequently, until browned. Stir in tomatoes, tomato purée and stock. Bring to the boil. Reduce heat, cover and simmer gently for 30 minutes. Season to taste with salt and pepper. Rinse eggplant slices under cold running water. Drain and pat dry with paper towels. Heat second measure of oil in a frying pan. Fry eggplant until light brown and soft. Place one-third of the eggplant in an ovenproof dish. Spread with half the meat mixture. Top with another third of eggplant and repeat with meat, finishing with eggplant. In a bowl combine egg yolks, flour and yoghurt. Season with salt and pepper. Spread on top of eggplant. Top with parmesan cheese. Cook at 180°C for 40 minutes or until golden. *Serves 6.*

# MUSHROOM RISOTTO

15 g dried porcini mushrooms
½ cup hot water
about 1.5 litres vegetable stock
¼ cup olive oil
1 onion, finely sliced
1 teaspoon crushed garlic
500 g arborio rice
½ cup dry white wine

2 tablespoons butter
150 g flat mushrooms, sliced
½ cup freshly grated parmesan cheese
salt and freshly ground black
   pepper to season
optional garnish: 4 rashers prosciutto
   or rindless bacon, chopped and
   cooked until crisp

Place porcini mushrooms in a bowl. Pour over the hot water and stand for 30 minutes. Bring stock to the boil in a saucepan. Heat oil in a heavy-based, deep-sided frying pan. Cook onion for 5 minutes until soft. Add garlic and rice and stir over a low heat for 2–3 minutes. Add wine and cook for 1 minute. Drain liquid from mushrooms and pour over the rice. Ladle over sufficient boiling stock to just cover the rice. Cook, stirring frequently, adding more stock to cover the rice as the liquid is absorbed. This will take about 18 minutes. While the rice is cooking, melt butter in a frying pan. Cook flat mushrooms for about 5 minutes or until the pan is dry. Remove risotto pan from the heat. Slice porcini mushrooms thinly. Add porcini and flat mushrooms and parmesan to the pan. Stir to combine. Cover pan and stand for 3–4 minutes. Season. Garnish with prosciutto or bacon. **Serves 4.** *(Below left)*

# MUSSELS IN TOMATO SAUCE

1 onion, chopped
1 cup dry white wine
36 mussels, scrubbed and beards removed
1 tablespoon butter
2 cloves garlic, crushed

1 tablespoon Champion standard
   grade flour
290 g can tomato purée
2 tablespoons chopped parsley
freshly ground black pepper

Put half the onion in a large frying pan. Add wine and bring to the boil. Add mussels. Cover and cook for about 8 minutes, until mussels open, removing them as they do. Discard any that do not open. Remove from heat. Drain, reserving ¾ cup of cooking liquid. Keep mussels warm. Melt butter in a saucepan. Add remaining onion and garlic. Cook for 5 minutes until onion is soft. Add flour and stir over a medium heat for 2 minutes. Remove from heat. Gradually add tomato purée and reserved cooking liquid. Return to heat, stirring constantly until sauce thickens and comes to the boil. Boil for 1 minute. Stir in parsley. Season to taste with pepper. Pour sauce over mussels. Serve with crusty French bread. **Serves 4–6.** *(Above right)*

# PASTA WITH PESTO, CRISPY BACON AND WALNUTS

400 g Diamond Italian Style Fettuccine
a little olive oil to cook
6 rashers lean rindless bacon,
    roughly chopped
1/2 cup Pesto (see page 182)
2 tablespoons olive oil

3/4 cup walnut pieces, toasted
1/2 cup grated parmesan cheese
freshly ground black pepper to season
sprigs of basil and shavings of parmesan
    cheese to garnish

Cook pasta according to packet instructions. Pour a little olive oil into a frying pan and heat. Cook bacon for 8–10 minutes until crisp and brown. Drain cooked pasta in a sieve. Return to saucepan and toss through all ingredients. Serve immediately. Garnish with sprigs of basil and parmesan cheese shavings. *Serves 4.*

# PENNE PASTA WITH BROCCOLI AND BLUE CHEESE SAUCE

*500 g Diamond Italian Style*
  *Penne pasta*
*1 tablespoon oil*
*1 onion, chopped*
*2 cloves garlic, crushed*

*1 head broccoli, cut into florets*
*300 ml cream*
*100 g blue cheese, crumbled*
*salt and freshly ground black pepper*

Cook pasta according to instructions on the packet. While the pasta is cooking, prepare the sauce. Heat oil in a frying pan. Cook onion for 5 minutes until soft. Add garlic and broccoli and cook for 3–4 minutes until broccoli is tender but still crunchy. Combine cream and cheese in a saucepan. Stir over a low heat until cheese melts and sauce is smooth. Stir in broccoli mixture. Drain pasta. Toss sauce through pasta. Season to taste with salt and pepper. Divide between 4 serving plates. Serve with a tossed salad and fresh bread. **Serves 4.** *(Below left)*

# PESTO AND BLUE CHEESE RIGATI

*400 g Diamond Italian Style*
  *Rigati pasta*
*2 tablespoons olive oil*
*1 onion, sliced*
*2 cloves garlic, crushed*

*¼ cup Pesto (see page 182)*
*200 g blue cheese, crumbled*
*freshly ground black pepper to season*
*shavings of parmesan cheese*
  *to garnish (optional)*

Cook pasta according to instructions on the packet. While pasta is cooking, heat oil in a frying pan. Cook onion and garlic for 5 minutes until soft. Stir in Pesto. Toss onion mixture, cheese and pepper through the cooked, drained pasta. Divide between 4 serving plates. Garnish with parmesan shavings. **Serves 4.** *(Above right)*

# PIZZA GALORE

## PIZZA DOUGH

1 tablespoon Edmonds active yeast
½ teaspoon sugar
1 cup tepid water

1 teaspoon salt
3 cups Champion high grade flour
1 tablespoon oil

Combine yeast, sugar and water in a bowl. Set aside for 15 minutes or until frothy. Combine salt and flour in a large bowl. Add yeast mixture and oil. Mix to a soft dough. Transfer to a lightly floured surface and knead for 5 minutes, until smooth and elastic. Place dough in a lightly oiled large bowl and cover with a teatowel. Stand in a warm place until doubled in bulk. Punch dough down in the centre, knead lightly for 1 minute and roll into a 30-cm-diameter circle. Place on a lightly greased oven tray. Top with ingredients of your choice. Cook at 220°C for 15 minutes or until well risen and golden. *Serves 4.*

N.B. To cook pizza on a pizza stone, transfer completed uncooked pizza to a heated pizza stone and cook as above.

## TOMATO SAUCE

1 tablespoon oil
1 onion, finely chopped
1 teaspoon crushed garlic
400 g can tomatoes in juice

2 tablespoons tomato paste
1 tablespoon chopped basil
salt and freshly ground black pepper

Heat oil in a frying pan. Cook onion for 5 minutes until soft. Add garlic, tomatoes and tomato paste, breaking up the tomatoes with a wooden spoon. Simmer for about 20 minutes until sauce is thick. Stir in basil. Season to taste. *(Top left)*

# TOPPING COMBINATIONS FOR PIZZA

### PIZZA SUPREME

Spread the prepared pizza base with *Tomato Sauce.* Top with *sliced salami, diced ham, anchovies, strips of roasted red capsicum, halved button mushrooms, pitted halved olives, thinly sliced red onion* and *grated mozzarella cheese.* *(Top right)*

### GREEK PIZZA

Spread the prepared pizza base with *Tomato Sauce.* Top with *diced feta cheese, pitted halved olives, thinly sliced red onion, strips of roasted red capsicum* and *grated mozzarella cheese.* *(Below left)*

### VEGETARIAN PIZZA

Spread the prepared pizza base with *herb pesto.* Top with *roasted sliced eggplant, thinly sliced red onion, crumbled feta cheese, sliced cherry tomatoes* and a scattering of *grated mozzarella cheese.* *(Middle right)*

### CHICKEN AND BLUE CHEESE PIZZA

Spread the prepared pizza base with *herb pesto.* Top with a little *grated cheddar cheese, shredded cooked chicken, crumbled blue cheese, chopped walnuts* and *halved cherry tomatoes.*

# DEEP-PAN PIZZA

*Pizza Dough (see page 107)*

### FILLING
*1 tablespoon oil*
*300 g lean beef mince*
*1 onion, finely chopped*
*1 teaspoon crushed garlic*
*400 g can tomatoes in juice*
*2 tablespoons tomato paste*

*salt and freshly ground black*
  *pepper to season*
*1 red capsicum, sliced*
*1 green or yellow capsicum, sliced*
*6 mushrooms, sliced*
*½ cup sliced pitted black olives, halved*
*¼ cup chopped sundried tomatoes*
*1 cup grated tasty cheddar cheese*
*¼ cup freshly grated parmesan cheese*

Roll out the risen dough on a lightly floured surface to a size to fit the base and halfway up the sides of a 22-cm-diameter springform tin. Brush the tin with oil and transfer the dough to the tin. To make the filling, heat the oil in a frying pan. Cook the mince and onion for 5 minutes until the mince has browned. Add the garlic, tomatoes in juice and tomato paste, breaking up the tomatoes with a wooden spoon. Cook for 25 minutes until the mixture is thick. Season. Cool. Spoon the mince mixture into prepared base. Arrange the capsicums, mushrooms, olives and sundried tomatoes on top of the mince. Sprinkle over cheeses. Bake at 200°C for 30 minutes until golden. Stand for 5 minutes before releasing from the sides of the tin and slicing into wedges. *Serves 4–6.*

# PORK AND NOODLE STIR-FRY

*500 g lean pork schnitzel*
*3 tablespoons hoisin sauce*
*¼ cup soy sauce*
*1 tablespoon honey*
*2 teaspoons crushed garlic*
*225 g dried egg noodles*
*2 tablespoons oil*

*2 onions, thinly sliced*
*½ cup water*
*2 bunches bok choy, sliced*
*1 tablespoon Edmonds Fielder's*
  *cornflour*
*1 tablespoon water*

Cut pork into 1-cm-wide strips. Combine hoisin sauce, soy sauce, honey and garlic in a bowl. Add pork and toss to combine. Cover and refrigerate for 1 hour. Cook noodles according to packet instructions. Tip into a sieve and refresh under cold running water. Heat 1 tablespoon of the oil in a wok or heavy-based frying pan. Drain meat from marinade, reserving the marinade. Stir-fry meat for 4–5 minutes until cooked through. Remove from wok. Add remaining oil to wok. Stir-fry onion for 4–5 minutes until soft. Combine reserved marinade and water and add to wok. Add pork, cooked noodles and bok choy, tossing over a medium heat for 1–2 minutes until heated through. Mix cornflour to a paste with water. Add to wok, stirring until mixture thickens. Serve immediately. *Serves 4.*

N.B. Shanghai choy may be used instead of bok choy.

# PORK AND SPINACH RISOTTO

*1 pork fillet (about 350 g)*
*2 tablespoons soy sauce*
*1 tablespoon dry sherry*
*1 tablespoon liquid honey*
*2 teaspoons sweet chilli sauce*
*about 1.5 litres beef stock*
*¼ cup olive oil*
*1 onion, finely sliced*

*1 teaspoon crushed garlic*
*500 g arborio rice*
*1 cup dry white wine*
*1 tablespoon olive oil*
*2 cups shredded spinach*
*½ cup freshly grated parmesan cheese*
*salt and freshly ground black*
  *pepper to season*

Trim visible fat from pork fillet. Place in a shallow glass or ceramic dish. Combine soy sauce, sherry, honey and chilli sauce. Pour over pork. Turn to coat evenly. Cover and refrigerate for at least 1 hour or up to 8 hours. Bring stock to the boil in a saucepan. Heat first measure of oil in a heavy-based, deep-sided frying pan. Cook onion for 5 minutes until soft. Add garlic and rice and stir over a low heat for 2–3 minutes to toast the rice. Add wine and cook for 1 minute. Ladle over sufficient boiling stock to just cover the rice. Cook, stirring frequently, adding more stock to cover the rice as the liquid is absorbed. (This will take about 18 minutes.) While rice is cooking, heat second measure of oil in a heavy-based frying pan. Drain pork from marinade. Cook meat over a medium-high heat, turning frequently, for about 12 minutes until cooked through. Remove from heat and allow meat to rest for 5 minutes before slicing thinly. Remove risotto pan from the heat. Add spinach, parmesan and sliced pork. Stir to combine. Cover pan and stand for 3–4 minutes. Season. Pile onto warm serving plates. ***Serves 4.***

# PUMPKIN AND LEEK RISOTTO

2 tablespoons butter
2 tablespoons olive oil
250 g peeled, seeded pumpkin,
    cut into 1-cm cubes
1 small leek, sliced and washed
1 teaspoon crushed garlic
about 1.5 litres chicken or vegetable stock

2 tablespoons olive oil
500 g arborio rice
½ cup dry white wine
½ cup freshly grated parmesan cheese
2 tablespoons chopped parsley
salt and freshly ground black
    pepper to taste

Combine butter and first measure of oil in a frying pan. Heat until butter melts. Add pumpkin, leek and garlic. Stir over a low heat for 2–3 minutes. Cover pan and continue cooking for 10–12 minutes, stirring occasionally, until pumpkin is tender. While vegetables are cooking, heat stock to boiling point in a saucepan. Heat second measure of oil in a heavy-based, deep-sided frying pan. Add rice to frying pan and stir over a low heat for 2–3 minutes to toast. Add wine and cook for 1 minute. Ladle over sufficient boiling stock to just cover the rice. Cook, stirring frequently, adding more stock to cover the rice as the liquid is absorbed. (This will take about 18 minutes.) Remove pan from the heat. Add cooked vegetables, parmesan and parsley. Stir gently to combine. Cover pan and stand for 3–4 minutes. Season. Pile onto warm serving plates. *Serves 4.*

# QUICK THAI GREEN CHICKEN CURRY

2 tablespoons Thai green curry paste
1 onion, thinly sliced
750 g boneless, skinless chicken,
    thinly sliced
1 cup coconut cream
1 tablespoon fish sauce
2 spring onions, thinly sliced

2 courgettes, thinly sliced
¼ teaspoon finely chopped,
    seeded red chilli
2 tablespoons roughly chopped
    coriander
cooked rice to serve

Heat a medium, heavy-based frying pan. Add curry paste and onion and cook for 1–2 minutes, stirring constantly, until paste is fragrant. Add chicken and cook for 4–5 minutes, stirring frequently. Add coconut cream and fish sauce and cook for a further 3–4 minutes, until chicken is cooked through. Stir through spring onions, courgettes, chilli and coriander. Serve immediately on a bed of cooked rice. ***Serves 4.*** *(Below left)*

# RICCIOLINI PASTA WITH PUMPKIN, FETA AND BASIL

1 tablespoon oil
1 onion, chopped
2 cloves garlic, crushed
1 teaspoon dried oregano
2 cups peeled, diced pumpkin
½ cup vegetable or chicken stock
300 g mushrooms, sliced

500 g Diamond Italian Style Ricciolini
    pasta
2 tablespoons olive oil
200 g feta cheese, diced
2 tablespoons chopped basil
salt and freshly ground black pepper

Heat oil in a frying pan. Cook onion for 5 minutes until clear. Add garlic, oregano, pumpkin and stock. Cook over a medium heat until pumpkin is tender. Add mushrooms and cook for 5–6 minutes until pan is dry. While vegetables are cooking, cook pasta according to the instructions on the packet. Drain. Toss vegetables, oil, feta and basil through drained pasta. Season to taste with salt and pepper. Serve with a tossed salad and bread. ***Serves 4.*** *(Above right)*

# SALMON RISSOLES

210 g can salmon
1 cup mashed potato
1 egg, lightly beaten
1 small onion, finely chopped
¾ cup Champion standard grade flour

2 teaspoons Edmonds baking powder
¼ cup chopped parsley
salt and freshly ground black pepper
Champion standard grade flour to dust
oil to cook

Drain and flake salmon, reserving liquid. Combine salmon, reserved liquid, potato, egg and onion. Sift flour and baking powder into salmon mixture. Add parsley and mix well. Season to taste with salt and pepper. Divide mixture into 8 even-sized portions. Shape into rounds and dust with flour. Heat a little oil in a large frying pan. Cook rissoles for 5 minutes on each side, until golden. Drain on paper towels. *Serves 4.* *(Below left)*

# SEAFOOD RISOTTO

about 1.5 litres chicken or fish stock
¼ cup olive oil
1 onion, finely chopped
2 cloves garlic, crushed
500 g arborio rice
1 cup dry white wine
250 g firm white fish fillets,
    cut into chunks
16 scallops (optional)

12 marinated mussels, drained
100 g cooked prawns or shrimps
½ cup freshly grated parmesan cheese
finely grated zest of 1 lemon
juice of 1 lemon
3 tablespoons chopped dill or parsley
salt and freshly ground black
    pepper to season

Bring stock to the boil in a saucepan. Heat oil in a heavy-based, deep-sided frying pan. Cook onion for 5 minutes until soft. Add garlic and rice and stir over a low heat for 2–3 minutes to toast the rice. Add ½ cup of wine and cook for 1 minute. Ladle over sufficient boiling stock to just cover the rice. Cook, stirring frequently, adding more stock to cover the rice as the liquid is absorbed. (This will take about 18 minutes.) Three to 4 minutes before the rice is cooked, bring remaining wine to the boil in a saucepan. Add fish chunks and cook for 1 minute, turning once. Add scallops, cook for a further minute until fish and scallops just turn white. The seafood will not be completely cooked at this stage. Remove from heat. Drain liquid from pan. Add all seafood, parmesan, lemon zest and juice to cooked rice. Toss gently to combine. Cover pan and stand for 3–4 minutes. Stir in dill. Season to taste with salt and pepper. Serve immediately on warm plates. *Serves 4.* *(Above right)*

# SPICED CHICKEN PILAF

2 single boneless, skinless
    chicken breasts
1 tablespoon oil
1 onion, finely chopped
2 cloves garlic, crushed
1½ cups basmati rice,
    thoroughly washed
2½ cups chicken stock
½ cup freshly squeezed orange juice

1 teaspoon turmeric
½ teaspoon ground cinnamon
2 bay leaves
3 spring onions, chopped
½ cup sliced almonds, toasted
2 tablespoons chopped parsley
salt and freshly ground black
    pepper to season

Cut chicken into bite-sized pieces. Heat oil in a heavy-based frying pan. Cook chicken and onion for about 5 minutes until onion is soft. Add garlic, rice, stock, orange juice, turmeric, cinnamon and bay leaves. Bring to the boil, stirring frequently. Reduce heat to low. Cover pan and simmer for about 20–25 minutes, stirring occasionally, until rice is cooked and the liquid is absorbed. Remove from heat. Remove bay leaves. Add spring onions, almonds and parsley. Stir to combine. Season to taste. **Serves 4.**

# STUFFED BAKED CAPSICUMS

1 tablespoon oil
1 onion, finely chopped
500 g lean beef mince
1 teaspoon ground cumin
400 g can tomatoes in juice
2 tablespoons tomato paste
2 cloves garlic, crushed

1 cup water
½ cup long grain rice, washed
¼ cup chopped parsley
salt and freshly ground black pepper
6 large (or 8 medium) capsicums,
    any colour

Heat oil in a frying pan. Cook onion, mince and cumin for 5 minutes or until meat has browned. Add tomatoes, breaking them up with a wooden spoon. Stir in tomato paste, garlic, water and rice. Simmer for 20–25 minutes until rice is cooked and sauce is thick. Add parsley. Season with salt and pepper. Cut tops off capsicums to form a lid. If necessary, shave a little off the base of capsicums so they stand upright. Remove seeds. Spoon rice-mince filling into capsicums. Place lid on top. Stand in an ovenproof baking dish. Pour in sufficient water to come 1 cm up the sides of the capsicums. Bake at 180°C for 30 minutes until tender. *Serves 3–4.*

# SUNDRIED TOMATO AND FETA-STUFFED CHICKEN BREASTS

*1 cup fresh white breadcrumbs*
*200 g feta cheese, crumbled*
*⅓ cup chopped sundried tomatoes*
*2 spring onions, sliced*
*1 tablespoon chopped rosemary*
*1 egg*

*salt and freshly ground black*
  *pepper to season*
*4 single boneless, skinless*
  *chicken breasts*
*12 rashers streaky rindless bacon*
*liquid honey to drizzle*

To make the stuffing, combine breadcrumbs, feta, sundried tomatoes, spring onions, rosemary, egg and salt and pepper in a bowl. Mix well. Trim visible fat from chicken. Place chicken between 2 sheets of plastic wrap. Pound with a heavy object (e.g. a rolling pin) to flatten to an even thickness of 6 mm. Cover half of each breast with stuffing, then fold over to enclose. Wrap 3 rashers of bacon around each parcel to cover. Place chicken in a baking dish. Drizzle over a little honey. Bake at 180°C for 25–30 minutes, basting chicken once or twice during this time. Turn oven to grill for 2–3 minutes to crisp the bacon. Stand for 4–5 minutes before cutting parcels into slices. Arrange slices of chicken on serving plates. Serve with vegetables of your choice, or a tossed salad. **Serves 4.**

# TANDOORI CHICKEN BREASTS

¾ cup natural unsweetened yoghurt
2 cloves garlic, crushed
1 tablespoon lemon juice
2 teaspoons grated root ginger
2 tablespoons paprika
1 teaspoon ground cumin
½ teaspoon ground cardamom

¼ teaspoon chilli powder
4 single boneless, skinless chicken breasts
cooked rice, naan bread or poppadoms,
   to serve
mango chutney, to serve
Cucumber and Mint Raita
   (see page 182), to serve

Combine yoghurt, garlic, lemon juice, ginger, paprika, cumin, cardamom and chilli powder in a bowl. Mix well. Trim visible fat from chicken. Place chicken between 2 sheets of plastic wrap. Pound with a heavy object (e.g. a rolling pin) until chicken is an even thickness — about 1 cm thick. Preheat oven grill. Place chicken in a single layer in a shallow roasting dish. Smother upper surface of chicken with half of the tandoori mixture. Grill for 6–8 minutes. Turn chicken and smother remaining side with tandoori mixture. Grill for a further 6–8 minutes until cooked through. Serve on a bed of cooked rice, accompanied by naan bread or poppadoms, mango chutney and Cucumber and Mint Raita. *Serves 4.* *(Middle left)*

# THAI-STYLE BEEF AND BABY CORN STIR-FRY

500 g lean fast-fry beef steak, e.g. rump,
   porterhouse, fillet
2 tablespoons vegetable oil
1 teaspoon crushed garlic
1 small red chilli, seeded
   and finely chopped
2 teaspoons Thai-style red curry paste

2 tablespoons fish sauce
2 tablespoons oyster sauce
2 x 425 g cans baby corn, drained
salt and freshly ground black pepper
¾ cup roasted peanuts
2 tablespoons chopped coriander
cooked rice to serve

Cut meat into narrow strips. Heat oil in wok or large heavy-based frying pan. Stir-fry beef, garlic and chilli over a high heat for 3–4 minutes. Add curry paste, fish sauce, oyster sauce and corn. Stir-fry for 2–3 minutes. Season with salt and pepper. Add peanuts and coriander and toss to combine. Serve on a bed of cooked rice. *Serves 4.* *(Below right)*

# TORRONCINI NAPOLITANA

1 tablespoon oil
1 onion, chopped
2 cloves garlic, crushed
1 teaspoon dried marjoram
1 teaspoon dried oregano
400 g can tomatoes in juice, chopped
¼ cup red wine

1 tablespoon tomato paste
1 tablespoon sugar
salt and freshly ground black
   pepper to season
500 g Diamond Italian Style
   Torroncini pasta
½ cup chopped basil

Heat oil in a frying pan. Cook onion for 5 minutes until soft. Add garlic, marjoram and oregano and cook for 2 minutes. Add tomatoes, wine and tomato paste. Simmer for 10 minutes. Add sugar. Season. Cook pasta according to the instructions on the packet. Drain. Stir basil into sauce, then toss sauce through the pasta. *Serves 4.* *(Top right)*

# DESSERTS

# BAKED LEMON CHEESECAKE

### BASE
1 cup plain biscuit crumbs
50 g butter, melted

### FILLING
500 g cream cheese, softened
250 g sour cream

1 cup caster sugar
2 tablespoons Champion standard
 grade flour
1 tablespoon finely grated lemon zest
¼ cup lemon juice
3 eggs, lightly beaten

To make the base, combine biscuit crumbs and butter. Mix well. Press evenly over the base of a 20-cm-diameter springform tin. Refrigerate while preparing the filling. Place cream cheese, sour cream, sugar, flour, lemon zest and juice in a food processor. Blend till smooth. With the motor running on slow speed, gradually add eggs, processing until well blended. Pour filling into tin. Bake at 150°C for 1 hour 50 minutes or until firm. Cool in tin. Cover and refrigerate for at least 6 hours before serving. *Serves 8–10.* *(Below left)*

# BANANA PANCAKES

1 cup Champion standard grade flour
½ teaspoon ground nutmeg
⅛ teaspoon salt
1 egg

about 1 cup milk
1 large banana, mashed
sliced banana to garnish
maple syrup to serve

Sift flour, nutmeg and salt into a bowl. Add egg, mixing to combine. Gradually beat in sufficient milk to mix to a smooth batter. Chill for 1 hour. Stir. The batter will thicken on standing. Stir in banana. Heat a greased pancake pan or small frying pan. Pour in just enough batter to cover base of pan. Cook until golden on underside. Release with knife around edges. Flip or turn and cook other side. Stack pancakes as you cook. To serve, fold pancakes into quarters. Place 2 pancakes on each serving plate. Garnish with sliced banana and drizzle with maple syrup. *Serves 4.* *(Above right)*

# CHEESEBOARDS

A cheeseboard makes a wonderful alternative to dessert. Cheeseboards can also be served before the dessert course, as the French do. Simplicity is the key to a well presented cheeseboard. The following guidelines will assist in achieving a superb result:

Offer 2 or 3 reasonable sized pieces of cheese rather than numerous small ones that will dry out quickly and look unappetising.

Select different types of cheese from the categories listed below, for an interesting presentation.

To ensure the cheeseboard is visually attractive, use different shaped cheeses, for example, a wedge, a log and a cylinder of cheese.

Remove cheese from the refrigerator at least 1 hour before serving. This allows the cheese to come back to room temperature where the flavour is best appreciated.

Keep garnishes simple — slices of crisp apple, a handful of quality shelled walnuts or a small bunch of grapes is all that is required.

Serve unsalted crackers or sliced French or walnut bread with the cheeseboard. Place them on a separate plate. (If placed directly alongside cheese, crackers can absorb moisture and become soft.)

# CHEESE CATEGORIES

### FRESH CHEESE
Fresh cheeses have a high moisture content and therefore a relatively short shelf life. They do not have a rind. Fresh cheeses include ricotta, fresh mozzarella, cream cheese, cottage cheese and feta.

### SOFT WHITE CHEESE
Covered with a white rind, soft white cheeses begin ripening from the outside. If the interior of the cheese is chalky in appearance, it is not completely ripe. When at its prime for eating, the interior should be creamy and soft. Examples include camembert and brie.

### SEMI-SOFT CHEESE
A springy texture is characteristic of semi-soft cheeses. They are often covered with a wax rind and are suited to use in cooking. Edam, gouda and raclette are semi-soft cheeses.

### HARD CHEESE
Hard cheeses mature slowly. The most common example is cheddar. Parmesan and gruyere also fall into this category. The texture of hard cheeses varies widely.

### BLUE CHEESE
Blue mould is added to the milk, then metal rods are used to pierce the cheese, allowing air to enter and thus encouraging the mould to grow.

### SPECIALTY CHEESES
This category includes any cheeses that have ingredients such as nuts, herbs or fruit flavourings.

# CHOCOLATE AND ALMOND STUFFED PEACHES

6 firm, ripe peaches
¼ cup freshly squeezed orange juice
100 g amaretti biscuits, crushed
¼ cup ground almonds
75 g dark chocolate, finely chopped
2 tablespoons melted butter
whipped cream or crème fraîche
    to serve

Cut peaches in half. Remove stones. Use 2 tablespoons of the orange juice to brush cut surfaces of peaches. Combine remaining orange juice with biscuit crumbs, almonds, chocolate and butter. Mix well. Pile mixture into peach cavities. Place on a baking tray. Bake at 200°C for 20 minutes until peaches are tender. Serve with whipped cream. *Serves 6.*

N.B. Gingernuts can be used as an alternative to amaretti biscuits.

# CHOCOLATE DESSERT CAKE

1 cup seedless raisins
1 cup water
½ cup freshly squeezed orange juice
1 teaspoon Edmonds baking soda
125 g butter, softened
¾ cup caster sugar
2 eggs
1 cup Champion standard grade flour
1 teaspoon Edmonds baking powder
½ cup cocoa

CHOCOLATE SAUCE
100 g dark chocolate, chopped
½ cup cream
2 tablespoons butter

orange zest to garnish

Combine raisins, water and orange juice in a small saucepan. Bring to the boil over a low heat. Remove from heat. Stir in baking soda. Cool slightly. Transfer to a food processor and blend to a smooth consistency. Cream butter and sugar until light and fluffy. Add eggs one at a time. Sift together flour, baking powder and cocoa. Fold dry ingredients and liquid ingredients alternately into creamed mixture. Transfer to a greased 22-cm-diameter cake tin that has had the base lined with baking paper. Bake at 180°C for 50–55 minutes or until cake springs back when lightly pressed. Cool in tin for 10 minutes before placing on a serving plate. Serve warm, drizzled with Chocolate Sauce and garnished with orange zest. To make the sauce, combine chocolate, cream and butter in a small saucepan. Stir over a low heat until chocolate and butter have melted and the sauce is smooth. *Serves 6–8.* *(Below right)*

N.B. As an alternative to the Chocolate Sauce, this cake is also delicious served with Raspberry Crème Fraîche Dip (see page 129).

# CHOCOLATE-GARNISHED HAZELNUT MERINGUE TORTE

8 egg whites
2 cups caster sugar
1 teaspoon DYC vinegar
1 teaspoon vanilla essence
1 tablespoon Edmonds Fielder's
    cornflour

½ cup roasted, shelled hazelnuts,
    finely chopped
2 tablespoons cocoa
whipped cream
whole hazelnuts and chocolate
    shavings to garnish

Preheat oven to 180°C. Draw three 20-cm-diameter circles on baking paper. Lay baking paper on oven trays. Using an electric mixer, beat egg whites and caster sugar for 10–15 minutes or until thick and glossy. Mix vinegar, essence and cornflour to a smooth paste. Add to meringue. Beat on high speed for a further 3 minutes. Fold in hazelnuts and cocoa. Divide meringue evenly between the 3 circles, spreading to within 2 cm of the edge. Place meringue circles in oven. Turn oven temperature down to 100°C. Bake for 70 minutes. Turn off oven. Open oven door slightly and leave meringues in oven until cold. Carefully lift a meringue disc onto a serving plate. Smother with whipped cream, then top with another meringue disc. Cover with more whipped cream and top with remaining meringue disc. Cover top of torte with whipped cream. Garnish with whole hazelnuts and chocolate shavings. *Serves 8.*

# COFFEE LIQUEUR CHEESECAKE

### BASE
*125 g plain sweet biscuits*
*¼ cup chopped walnuts*
*75 g butter, melted*

### FILLING
*2 teaspoons instant coffee*
*¼ cup boiling water*
*3 tablespoons coffee liqueur, e.g.*
  *Tia Maria, Bailey's Irish Cream*

*500 g cream cheese, softened*
*½ cup caster sugar*
*½ cup (125 g) sour cream*
*4 teaspoons gelatine*
*300 ml cream, lightly whipped*

*whipped cream, chocolate-coated*
  *coffee beans (or grated chocolate),*
  *to garnish*

Place biscuits and walnuts in a food processor. Pulse until reduced to a coarse crumb. Add butter and pulse until combined. Press crumb mixture over the base of a greased 20-cm-diameter springform tin that has had the base lined with baking paper. Refrigerate while preparing the filling. In a small bowl, dissolve coffee in the boiling water. Stir in liqueur. Set aside to cool. Using an electric mixer, beat cream cheese and sugar until smooth. Add sour cream and beat until combined. Sprinkle gelatine over cooled coffee mixture. Sit the bowl over a bowl of hot water and stir until gelatine has dissolved. Using a large metal spoon, fold coffee mixture into cream cheese. Fold in whipped cream. Pour filling over prepared base. Cover and refrigerate for 6 hours. Decorate with whipped cream and chocolate-coated coffee beans. ***Serves 8–10.*** *(Below left)*

# FRESH SUMMER FRUIT PLATTER
## WITH RASPBERRY CRÈME FRAÎCHE DIP

*1 cup fresh or frozen raspberries*
*1 tablespoon lemon juice*
*2 tablespoons icing sugar*
*300 g crème fraîche*

*selection of fresh summer fruit,*
  *e.g. peaches, apricots, nectarines,*
  *melon, strawberries, bananas,*
  *new season's apples*

To make the dip, place raspberries, lemon juice and icing sugar in a food processor. Pulse until raspberries are broken down. Transfer to a bowl and fold in crème fraîche. Refrigerate until required. To serve, place dip in a bowl in the centre of a platter. Surround with sliced fruit. *(Above right)*

N.B. Strawberries may be used as an alternative to raspberries for the dip. Cut strawberries in half before placing in food processor.

# ICE-CREAM

*4 eggs, separated*
*¼ cup caster sugar*
*¼ cup caster sugar*

*1 teaspoon vanilla essence*
*300 ml cream, whipped*

Beat egg whites until stiff peaks form. Gradually add first measure of sugar, 1 tablespoon at a time, beating until sugar dissolves before adding the next tablespoon. In a separate bowl beat egg yolks and second measure of sugar until thick and pale. Add essence. Gently fold yolk mixture into egg white mixture. Fold cream into egg mixture. Pour mixture into a shallow container suitable for freezing. Freeze for 2 hours or until firm. *Serves 6.* (Top right)

## VARIATIONS

Any of the following can be added after the cream:
*1 cup chocolate chips*
*1 cup chopped nuts*
*1 cup puréed berry fruit, e.g. strawberries, raspberries*

# ICE-CREAM TERRINE — CHOCOLATE AND APRICOT

### CHOCOLATE ICE-CREAM
*100 g dark chocolate, chopped, or melts*
*250 ml cream*
*3 eggs, separated*
*¼ cup caster sugar*

### APRICOT ICE-CREAM
*¾ cup dried apricots, roughly chopped*
*⅓ cup freshly squeezed orange juice*
*¼ cup brandy (or freshly squeezed orange juice)*
*3 eggs, separated*
*½ cup caster sugar*
*250 ml cream, whipped*

*optional garnish: chocolate curls and sliced apricots*

To make the chocolate ice-cream, place chocolate and a ¼ cup of the cream in a double boiler or heatproof bowl. Sit the bowl over a saucepan of simmering water. Stir continuously until the chocolate melts and the mixture is smooth. Cool slightly. Using an electric mixer, beat yolks and sugar until thick and pale. Add chocolate and beat until combined. Whip remaining cream. Fold cream into chocolate mixture. Beat egg whites until soft peaks form. Fold chocolate mixture into egg whites. Transfer to a 20-cm-diameter springform tin, levelling the top with the back of a spoon. Cover and freeze for 4 hours.

To make the apricot ice-cream, combine apricots and orange juice in a small saucepan. Stir over a medium heat until the juice is absorbed. Cool slightly. Place in a food processor with brandy and blend until smooth. Using an electric mixer, beat yolks and sugar until thick and pale. Beat in apricot purée. Beat egg whites until soft peaks form. Fold cream, then egg whites, into yolk mixture. Spoon over frozen chocolate ice-cream. Cover and freeze for a further 4 hours. To serve, cut into wedges. Garnish with chocolate curls and sliced apricots. *Serves 8.* (Below right)

# INDIVIDUAL PINEAPPLE AND GINGER STEAMED PUDDINGS

melted butter to grease
2 tablespoons golden syrup
1 tablespoon butter
440 g can pineapple rings
    in syrup, drained
100 g butter
1/3 cup golden syrup
1/3 cup sugar

1 1/2 cups Champion standard
    grade flour
1 teaspoon Edmonds baking soda
1 1/2 teaspoons ground ginger
1 egg, lightly beaten
1/4 cup milk

custard or whipped cream to serve

Thoroughly grease six 9-cm-diameter ramekins with melted butter. Place first measure of golden syrup and butter in a small saucepan. Stir over a low heat until butter has melted. Brush syrup over the base of the ramekins. Place a pineapple ring in the base of each ramekin. Combine second measure of butter, golden syrup and sugar in a saucepan. Stir over a low heat until butter has melted and mixture is smooth. Remove from heat. Sift together flour, baking soda and ginger. Make a well in the centre of dry ingredients. Pour in butter mixture. Beat lightly with a wooden spoon until ingredients are almost incorporated. Add egg and milk and mix well. Divide batter between the ramekins. Pour hot water into a roasting dish to a level of 3 cm. Sit ramekins in the water. Cover roasting dish tightly with foil. Bake at 180°C for 30 minutes or until a skewer inserted in the centre of a pudding comes out clean. Stand for 5 minutes before serving. To serve each pudding, run a knife around the inside of the ramekin. Place a serving plate over the ramekin and invert — the pudding should drop out. Serve with custard or cream. **Serves 6.** *(Below left)*

# PASSIONFRUIT FLAN

Sweet Shortcrust Pastry (see page 180)

### FILLING
4 eggs, lightly beaten
1/2 cup passionfruit pulp (about 6 passionfruit)
3/4 cup caster sugar
2 tablespoons Champion standard grade flour
3/4 cup cream

whipped cream and passionfruit pulp to serve

Roll chilled pastry out on a lightly floured surface to fit a 24-cm-diameter flan tin. Line tin with pastry. Cut off excess pastry. Freeze pastry case for 5 minutes. Bake blind (see Glossary page 186) at 190°C for 15 minutes. Remove baking blind material and return to oven for 2–3 minutes to dry out the base. Turn down oven to 160°C. While pastry case is cooking, prepare the filling. Whisk all filling ingredients together in a bowl. Pour passionfruit filling into pastry case. Bake for 45–50 minutes or until filling is set. Serve at room temperature accompanied by whipped cream, drizzled with a little passionfruit pulp. **Serves 8.** *(Top left)*

# PAVLOVA ROLL WITH APRICOT FILLING

5 egg whites
1 cup caster sugar
1 teaspoon Edmonds Fielder's cornflour
1 teaspoon vanilla essence
1 teaspoon DYC white vinegar
icing sugar to dust

### APRICOT FILLING
400 g can apricots in light syrup
300 ml cream, lightly whipped

Using an electric mixer, beat egg whites and sugar for 10–15 minutes until thick and glossy. Mix cornflour to a paste with essence and vinegar. Add to meringue. Beat on high speed for a further 5 minutes. While meringue is being beaten, prepare the tin. Thoroughly grease a 20 x 30 cm shallow baking tin. Line the base and sides with baking paper. Grease the baking paper. Preheat oven to 160°C. Spread meringue evenly over the base of the baking tin. Bake for 20 minutes until pale golden on top. The centre should be slightly soft. Remove from oven and stand for 5 minutes. Cut a piece of baking paper slightly longer than the baking tin. Lay on a flat surface. Dust thoroughly with icing sugar. Invert meringue onto the dusted paper. Peel off baking paper on the bottom of the meringue. Working quickly, roll meringue into a log, including the baking paper in the roll. Set aside to cool completely. To make the filling, drain apricots thoroughly. Place in a food processor and blend to a purée. Fold together whipped cream and apricot purée. Carefully unroll the meringue. Spread apricot filling evenly over the unrolled surface. Roll up into a log and serve immediately. To serve, cut into slices. **Serves 8.**

# PEAR, APPLE AND GINGER CRUMBLE WITH CUSTARD

3 apples, peeled, quartered,
    cored and sliced
3 pears, peeled, quartered,
    cored and sliced
3/4 cup brown sugar
1 teaspoon cinnamon
1 tablespoon water

### CRUMBLE
2 cups Fleming's rolled oats
1 cup Champion standard grade flour
1 cup brown sugar
1½ teaspoons ground ginger
100 g butter, melted

custard to serve

Arrange fruit in a large ovenproof baking dish. Sprinkle over sugar, cinnamon and water. Combine crumble ingredients in a bowl. Mix well. Sprinkle over fruit. Press lightly with the back of a spoon. Bake at 180°C for 45 minutes. Serve with custard. **Serves 6–8.**

# SPICED PUMPKIN PIE

### PASTRY

1¼ cups Champion standard grade flour
¼ cup icing sugar
100 g cold butter, chopped
1 egg yolk
1–2 tablespoons cold water

### FILLING

500 g peeled, seeded crown pumpkin
¾ cup golden syrup
4 eggs, lightly beaten
½ cup cream
1 teaspoon cinnamon
¼ teaspoon ground nutmeg
whipped or clotted cream to serve

To make pastry, sift the flour and icing sugar into a bowl. Rub butter into the flour until mixture resembles coarse breadcrumbs. Add yolk and enough water to mix to a stiff dough. (Pastry can be made in a food processor.) Gather the dough into a ball, cover with plastic wrap and refrigerate for 30 minutes. To prepare the filling, chop pumpkin into chunks. Boil or microwave until tender. Drain well, then mash. While the pumpkin is still hot, stir in golden syrup. Mix well. Cool, then stir in remaining ingredients. Roll dough out on a lightly floured surface to fit a 24-cm-diameter, 3.5-cm-deep flan tin. Transfer dough to tin and trim off any excess. Prick the base. Refrigerate pastry base for 10 minutes, then freeze for 5 minutes. Bake blind (see Glossary page 186) at 190°C for 12 minutes. Remove baking blind material and return to oven for 3–4 minutes to dry out pastry base. Reduce oven temperature to 180°C. Pour filling into pastry case. Bake for 45 minutes until filling has set. Serve warm with cream. *Serves 8. (Below left)*

# UPSIDE-DOWN PUDDING

125 g butter
½ cup sugar
2 eggs
1 cup Champion standard grade flour
2 teaspoons Edmonds baking powder

2 tablespoons milk
25 g butter, melted
¼ cup brown sugar
1 teaspoon mixed spice
2 x 425 g cans pear halves, drained

Cream first measure of butter and sugar until light and fluffy. Add eggs one at a time, beating well after each addition. Sift flour and baking powder together. Fold into creamed mixture. Stir in milk. Combine second measure of butter, sugar and mixed spice. Spread this mixture onto the base of a 20-cm-diameter cake tin. Arrange pears, cut side down, on the butter mixture. Spoon cake mixture over fruit. Bake at 180°C for 40 minutes or until cake springs back when lightly touched. Unmould onto a serving plate. *Serves 6. (Above right)*

# WARM GINGERBREAD DATE CAKE

*1 cup pitted dates, roughly chopped*
*1½ cups water*
*¾ teaspoon Edmonds baking soda*
*2 eggs*
*¾ cup brown sugar*
*½ cup vegetable oil*
*¼ cup golden syrup*

*¼ cup chopped crystallised ginger*
*2½ cups Champion standard grade flour*
*2 tablespoons cocoa*
*1 teaspoon Edmonds baking powder*
*2 teaspoons ground ginger*
*icing sugar to dust*
*whipped cream to serve*

Combine dates and water in a small saucepan. Bring to the boil. Remove from heat and stir in baking soda. Cool for 10 minutes. In a large bowl, whisk together eggs, sugar, oil, golden syrup and crystallised ginger. Sift together flour, cocoa, baking powder and ground ginger. Stir date mixture into egg mixture. Lastly, fold in dry ingredients. Spoon into a greased 22-cm-diameter cake tin that has been lined with baking paper. Bake at 180°C for 50–55 minutes or until a skewer inserted in the centre of the cake comes out clean. Stand for 10 minutes before turning onto a wire rack. Serve warm or cold, dusted with icing sugar and accompanied by cream. *(Below left)*

# ZUCCOTTO

*400 g sponge cake (2 cm thick)*
*½ cup Cointreau or Maraschino or*
   *Grand Marnier to brush*
*500 ml cream, lightly whipped*
*100 g dark chocolate, or melts, melted*
   *and cooled slightly*

*½ cup chocolate chips*
*¼ cup finely chopped red glacé cherries*
*¼ cup finely chopped glacé pineapple*
*⅓ cup chopped, roasted,*
   *shelled hazelnuts*
*cocoa to dust*

Line a 6-cup capacity basin with plastic wrap so it extends over sides of basin. Cut sponge into 1.5-cm-wide strips, tapering them at the ends, so they are long enough to line the basin. Brush sponge strips with liqueur. Line basin with sponge, reserving some for top of pudding. Brush sponge lining the basin with more liqueur to completely soak. Divide cream equally between 2 bowls. Fold one portion into the melted chocolate, one tablespoon at a time. Cover sponge with chocolate mixture, leaving a cavity. Cover and refrigerate for 2 hours. Fold chocolate chips, cherries, pineapple and hazelnuts into remaining cream. Spoon into cavity. Brush remaining sponge strips with liqueur and arrange over filling to cover. Cover with plastic wrap that is overhanging the basin. Weight with a heavy object. Refrigerate for 8 hours or overnight. To remove from basin, unfold plastic wrap and place a serving dish over the bowl. Carefully invert bowl to release pudding. Remove plastic wrap. Dust with sifted cocoa. **Serves 8.** *(Above right)*

# FESTIVE AND TRADITIONAL FARE

CHRISTMAS

# CHRISTMAS DINNER MENU 1
## (SERVES 6)

## ROAST CHICKEN
### WITH WILD RICE AND CASHEW NUT STUFFING

### STUFFING

*½ cup wild rice*
*1 tablespoon oil*
*1 onion, finely chopped*
*1 teaspoon crushed garlic*
*100 g button mushrooms, sliced*
*½ cup fresh breadcrumbs*
*½ cup (70 g) roughly chopped*
  *roasted cashew nuts*

*1 egg*
*salt and freshly ground black*
  *pepper to season*
*1 x No. 18 chicken*
*gravy, to serve*

To make the stuffing, cook rice in boiling water, or microwave until tender. Tip into a sieve. Refresh under cold running water. Drain thoroughly. While the rice is cooking, heat oil in a frying pan. Cook onion for 5 minutes until soft. Add garlic and mushrooms and cook for 6–8 minutes until pan is dry. Combine all stuffing ingredients in a bowl. Mix well. Remove giblets from chicken. (If desired use to make gravy or stock.) Rinse out cavity with cold running water. Drain. Pat chicken dry with paper towels. Spoon stuffing into cavity. Close the cavity using a wooden skewer. Cross legs of chicken and tie with string, including the parson's nose, so the legs are neatly placed over the chicken. Bake at 180°C for 2 hours or until juices run clear. Remove from oven and stand for 5–10 minutes in a warm place before carving. Serve with gravy. *(Top right)*

## VEGETABLES

### ROAST VEGETABLES

To prepare for roasting, peel vegetables such as **potatoes**, **kumara** and **parsnip**. Seed **pumpkin**. Cut vegetables into chunks. One hour before the chicken is cooked, add vegetables to the roasting pan, turning to coat with pan juices. For a golden-brown finish to the vegetables, turn oven to grill for 3–4 minutes once the chicken has been removed. *(Top left)*

### STEAMED VEGETABLES

Choose a selection of the following seasonal vegetables to accompany the roast vegetables: **carrots**, **beans**, **asparagus**, **broccoli**, **brussels sprouts**. Bring a little water to the boil in a saucepan and steam vegetables until just tender. Drain. *(Middle)*

# CHRISTMAS DINNER MENU 2
## (SERVES 6)

## HOT ORANGE-GLAZED HAM ON THE BONE

cooked ham on the bone
whole cloves
½ cup orange marmalade

juice of 1 orange
¼ cup brown sugar
2 tablespoons sherry

Remove rind from ham by cutting through the skin at the shank-end with a small knife. Make an incision lengthwise down the middle of the rind, starting from the shank-end cut. Insert thumb under the incision and ease rind off one half of ham. Repeat with other side. Trim off any excess fat. Using a small sharp knife, score fat on the diagonal to a depth of 2 mm, then crossways to make diamonds. Push a clove into the centre of each diamond. Cover shank end with foil. Place ham on a rack in a large roasting dish. Combine marmalade, orange juice, brown sugar and sherry in a small saucepan. Stir over a medium heat until sugar has dissolved and glaze comes to the boil. Reduce heat and simmer for 5 minutes, stirring occasionally. Spoon half the glaze thickly over the ham, covering exposed fat. Bake at 160°C, allowing 10 minutes per 500 g. Baste 3–4 times during the cooking with remaining glaze. Set aside for 10 minutes before carving. *(Below left)*

N.B. To store leftover ham, cover with a clean damp teatowel and refrigerate. Change the teatowel daily.

## PAWPAW AND CORIANDER SALSA

½ pawpaw, seeded and peeled
2 spring onions, finely chopped
2 tablespoons chopped coriander

1 tablespoon lemon juice
freshly ground black pepper to season

Chop pawpaw into small cubes. Put all ingredients into a glass or ceramic bowl. Stir gently to combine. Cover and refrigerate for at least 30 minutes before serving. This salsa can be made up to 1 day before required. *(Above right)*

# MEDLEY OF SUMMER VEGETABLES

*4 capsicums, any colour*
*6 small courgettes*
*6 scallopini (optional)*
*18 asparagus spears*

*100 g green beans*
*3 tablespoons olive oil*
*rock salt or sea salt to sprinkle*
*Aioli (see below)*

Prepare vegetables. Cut capsicums in half, remove core and seeds, then cut in half again. Trim ends from courgettes, then cut in half lengthwise. Cut scallopini in half. Snap woody ends off asparagus. Trim beans. Preheat oven to 220°C. Pour oil into a roasting dish. Heat dish in oven for 5 minutes. Add vegetables and toss to coat with oil. Sprinkle with salt. Return pan to oven. Cook vegetables until just tender, turning frequently. The vegetables will cook at different rates — transfer to a warm dish when done. Serve accompanied by Aioli. *(Below left)*

# AIOLI

*2 egg yolks*
*1 teaspoon crushed garlic*
*1 tablespoon lemon juice*

*1 cup olive oil*
*salt and freshly ground black*
*pepper to season*

Place yolks, garlic and lemon juice in a food processor. Blend until smooth. With the motor running, gradually add oil, a little at a time. The mixture will thicken. (If the oil is added too quickly, the aioli will curdle.) Season to taste. ***Makes 1 cup.*** Serve, chilled, with medley of Summer Vegetables.

N.B. The Aioli may become very thick when refrigerated. For a more manageable consistency, add a little more lemon juice before serving. *(Above left)*

# MINTED BABY POTATOES

*new baby potatoes, scrubbed*
*3–4 sprigs mint*
*knob of butter*

Cook potatoes with the mint in boiling water until they are tender. Drain. Remove mint. Add butter and toss lightly until butter melts and potatoes are evenly coated. *(Above right)*

# CHRISTMAS COOKIES

125 g butter, softened
¾ cup caster sugar
1 egg
1 teaspoon vanilla essence

2 cups Champion standard grade flour
½ teaspoon Edmonds baking powder
¼ cup cocoa
narrow ribbon to hang biscuits

Cream butter and sugar until light and fluffy. Add egg. Beat well. Beat in essence. Sift flour, baking powder and cocoa. Stir into creamed mixture, mixing to a soft dough. Shape dough into a ball. Cover with plastic wrap and refrigerate for 30 minutes. Roll dough out on a floured surface to a thickness of 5 mm. Using Christmas-shaped biscuit cutters, stamp out shapes. Place on greased oven trays. Using a metal or wooden skewer, make a small hole in the top of each biscuit. Bake at 180°C for 12 minutes. Cool on wire racks. To hang the biscuits from the Christmas tree, thread ribbon through the hole in the top of each biscuit, tying the ends together.

N.B. The biscuits will not stay fresh for longer than 1 day, hanging from the tree. *(Below left)*

# HAZELNUT CHOCOLATE TRUFFLES

250 g dark chocolate, chopped (or melts)
25 g butter, chopped
½ cup cream
1 tablespoon Frangelico liqueur
    (optional)

¼ cup ground roasted hazelnuts
200 g dark chocolate, chopped (or melts)
21 hazelnuts, halved, to garnish

Place chocolate and butter in the top of a double boiler or a heatproof bowl. Place over simmering water. Stir constantly until chocolate melts and the mixture is smooth. Remove from heat. Stir in cream, liqueur and ground hazelnuts. Cover and refrigerate for several hours until firm. Roll teaspoons of mixture into balls. Place in a single layer on a plate. Cover with plastic wrap and refrigerate for 1 hour. To coat truffles, melt second measure of chocolate as above. Cool slightly. Quickly dip truffles into the melted chocolate, using a dipping stick or teaspoons. Allow excess chocolate to drain off. Place on a sheet of foil. Garnish each truffle with half a hazelnut. Allow to dry before storing in a covered container in a cool place. **Makes 42.** *(Above right)*

# LEMON STAR BISCUITS

125 g butter, softened
3/4 cup caster sugar
1 egg
2 teaspoons finely grated lemon zest
2 cups Champion standard grade flour

### LEMON ICING

1 cup icing sugar
2 teaspoons butter, softened
1 tablespoon lemon juice
boiling water to mix
silver balls to decorate (optional)

Cream butter and caster sugar until light and fluffy. Add egg and lemon zest. Beat well. Sift flour. Stir into creamed mixture, mixing to a soft dough. Shape dough into a ball. Cover with plastic wrap and refrigerate for 30 minutes. Roll dough out on a floured surface to a thickness of 5 mm. Using a star-shaped biscuit cutter, stamp out shapes. Place on greased oven trays. Bake at 180°C for 12 minutes until lightly golden. Cool on wire racks. To make icing, sift icing sugar into a bowl. Mix in butter and lemon juice. Add just enough water to achieve a spreadable consistency. When biscuits are cold, spread with Lemon Icing and decorate with silver balls. *(Below left)*

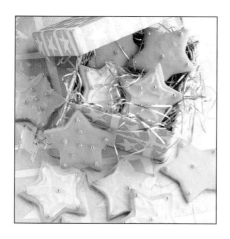

# PANFORTE

1 cup hazelnuts, toasted
   and roughly chopped
1 cup blanched almonds, toasted and
   roughly chopped
1/2 cup dried figs, chopped
1/2 cup dried apricots, chopped
1/4 cup crystallised ginger, chopped

1/4 cup mixed peel
3/4 cup Champion high grade flour
1 teaspoon cinnamon
3/4 teaspoon ground nutmeg
1/4 teaspoon ground cloves
1/2 cup liquid honey
1/2 cup caster sugar

Thoroughly grease a 20-cm-diameter cake tin. Line the base and sides with baking paper. Combine nuts, dried fruit, flour and spices in a mixing bowl. Mix well. Place honey and sugar in a small saucepan. Stir over a low heat until sugar dissolves. Bring to the boil, stirring constantly. Boil for about 2 minutes until mixture reaches the soft-ball stage. (To test for soft-ball stage, drop a small amount of mixture off a teaspoon into cold water. When a soft-ball forms, the mixture is ready. On a sugar thermometer, the soft-ball stage is 116°C.) Do not let the syrup change colour. Remove from the heat and let the bubbles subside. Carefully pour syrup over dry ingredients, then quickly mix to combine. Press into prepared tin. (Speed is vital, as the mixture will become sticky and unmanageable very quickly.) Bake at 150°C for 45 minutes in the lower third of the oven. Cool in tin. Wrap in foil and store in the refrigerator. To serve, cut into thin wedges. *(Above right)*

# PANETTONE

1 teaspoon sugar
1/4 cup warm water
4 teaspoons Edmonds active yeast
3/4 cup milk
75 g butter
4 cups Champion high grade flour
1/3 cup sugar

1/2 teaspoon salt
4 egg yolks, lightly beaten
3/4 cup sultanas
1/4 cup mixed peel
finely grated zest of 1 lemon
milk to brush

Dissolve first measure of sugar in warm water. Sprinkle yeast over water. Set aside in a warm place for 10 minutes until frothy. Place milk and butter in a small saucepan. Stir over a low heat until butter melts. Transfer to a large bowl and allow to cool to lukewarm. Stir in frothy yeast mixture. Using a wooden spoon, beat in 1 cup of the flour, and the sugar and salt. Cover with plastic wrap and stand in a warm place until mixture is bubbly. Mix yolks and remaining flour into the yeast mixture. Add sultanas, mixed peel and lemon zest. Mix to a soft dough with a wooden spoon. Turn dough onto a floured surface and knead for 10 minutes until smooth and elastic. Place dough in a lightly oiled bowl, turning to coat with oil. Cover with plastic wrap. Stand in a warm place until doubled in bulk (about 1½ hours). Punch dough down with a fist, then knead for 1 minute on a lightly floured surface. Form into a large ball and place in a greased, deep, 20-cm-diameter cake tin that has had the base lined with baking paper. Cover with plastic wrap and stand in a warm place until doubled in bulk. Brush top of risen Panettone with milk. Bake in the lower third of the oven at 200°C for 15 minutes, then reduce heat to 180°C and bake for a further 30 minutes or until bread sounds hollow when tapped. Leave in tin for 10 minutes before transferring to a wire rack to cool. To serve, cut into wedges. Serve buttered.

N.B. Panettone is best eaten on the day it is made. However, it will keep for up to 4 days. It is delicious toasted.

# STAINED-GLASS-WINDOW LOG

¾ cup Brazil nuts, toasted
and roughly chopped
10 red glacé cherries, halved
10 green glacé cherries, halved
12 dried apricots, quartered

250 g dark chocolate, roughly
chopped (or melts)
½ cup sweetened condensed milk
3 tablespoons cream

Combine nuts and dried fruit in a bowl. Place chocolate, condensed milk and cream in the top of a double boiler or heatproof bowl. Place over simmering water. Stir constantly until chocolate melts and mixture is smooth. Remove from heat. Add nut and fruit mixture. Mix well. Lay a 45 cm length of foil on a flat surface. Transfer chocolate mixture to the centre of the foil. Fold the foil over the mixture, then roll into a log about 35 cm long. Twist the ends of the foil to enclose the log. Refrigerate for 3–4 hours until firm. To serve, cut into slices. Store in the refrigerator. *(Below left)*

# TIRAMISÙ TERRINE

3 teaspoons instant coffee
¾ cup boiling water
¼ cup brandy
250 g packet sponge fingers
(savoiardi biscuits)
100 g dark chocolate, chopped (or melts)

300 ml cream
1 teaspoon gelatine
1 tablespoon cold water
¼ cup icing sugar
300 g mascarpone cheese
10–12 whole strawberries, hulled

Dissolve coffee in boiling water. Stir in brandy. Line an 11 x 21 cm loaf tin with plastic wrap so that it extends over the side of the tin. One by one, quickly dip 8 biscuits into the coffee mixture. Line the base of the tin with the biscuits. Keep remaining coffee mixture. Combine chocolate and ¼ cup of the cream in the top of a double boiler or heatproof bowl. Place over simmering water. Stir constantly until chocolate melts and the mixture is smooth. Remove from heat. Sprinkle gelatine over cold water. Place over a bowl of hot water and stir until gelatine dissolves. Stir into chocolate. Whip remaining cream and icing sugar together. Place mascarpone in a medium bowl. Beat with a wooden spoon until smooth. Fold in cream and chocolate. Spoon half the mixture evenly over biscuits. Place the strawberries in a line down the middle of the chocolate mixture. Carefully spoon over remaining chocolate mixture. Dip 9 more biscuits in reserved coffee mixture. Arrange on top of chocolate layer to cover completely. Fold plastic wrap over the terrine. Refrigerate for 4 hours. To serve, unfold plastic wrap from the top of the terrine. Invert onto a board or flat surface. Using a sharp knife, cut into slices. *Serves 6–8. (Above right)*

EASTER

# APRICOT-STUFFED FOREQUARTER

*1 kg boned lamb forequarter*
*¹/₂ cup chopped dried apricots*
*³/₄ cup soft breadcrumbs*

*3 tablespoons chopped parsley*
*1 tablespoon grated root ginger*
*freshly ground black pepper to season*

Open out meat and place on a flat surface, skin side down. Combine apricots, breadcrumbs, parsley, ginger and pepper. Spread stuffing over the flesh of the meat then roll up like a sponge roll. Secure with string. Place in a roasting pan or oven bag. Cook at 160°C for 1¹/₂ hours or until juices run clear when tested with a skewer. Serve hot or cold. *Serves 6. (Below left)*

# EASTER BISCUITS

*125 g butter, softened*
*¹/₂ cup sugar*
*¹/₂ teaspoon vanilla essence*
*1 tablespoon lemon juice*
*1¹/₂ cups Champion standard*
  *grade flour*

*1 teaspoon Edmonds baking powder*
*¹/₄ cup currants*
*¹/₄ cup mixed peel*
*melted chocolate for dipping*

Cream butter and sugar until light and fluffy. Beat in essence and lemon juice. Sift together flour and baking powder. Fold dry ingredients and fruit into creamed mixture. Roll heaped teaspoonfuls of mixture into balls. Place on greased baking trays. Press biscuits flat with the palm of your hand. Bake at 180°C for about 20 minutes or until biscuits are golden. Transfer to cake racks to cool. When biscuits are cold, dip into melted chocolate to coat half of the biscuit. Place on a sheet of foil until chocolate sets. Store in an airtight container. *Makes 20. (Above right)*

# TRADITIONAL
# FARE

# OLD-FASHIONED VEGETABLE SOUP

1 kg beef bones, fat removed
4 litres water
½ cup red lentils
½ cup pearl barley

½ cup split peas
2 cups vegetables, peeled and chopped,
    e.g. carrots, potatoes, parsnips
salt and freshly ground black pepper

Put bones, water, lentils, barley and split peas in a large saucepan. Bring to the boil and simmer for 2–3 hours until meat is falling off the bones. Remove bones, fat and gristle from the soup. Add vegetables. Cook for 35–40 minutes. Season to taste with salt and pepper. *Serves 8–10.* *(Top left)*

# PEA AND HAM SOUP

500 g bacon or ham bones
250 g split peas
1 medium onion, finely chopped

1 teaspoon salt
3 litres water
freshly ground black pepper to season

Put all ingredients in a large saucepan. Simmer slowly for 2–3 hours until peas are soft. For a very creamy soup, remove bones and purée soup in a blender or push through a sieve. Cut meat from bones and return to soup. *Serves 6.* *(Below right)*

# SPINACH AND CHEESE SOUFFLÉ

melted butter to grease dishes
2 cups shredded spinach, washed
2 tablespoons water
3 tablespoons butter
3 tablespoons Champion standard
    grade flour
1 cup milk
1 cup grated tasty cheddar cheese
1 teaspoon cayenne pepper
pinch of nutmeg
salt and freshly ground black pepper
4 eggs, separated

Thoroughly brush a 15-cm-diameter soufflé dish or four 10-cm-diameter soufflé dishes with melted butter. Place spinach and water in a saucepan. Cover and cook over a medium heat just until spinach wilts — about 2 minutes. Drain in a sieve. Refresh under cold running water. Squeeze out excess liquid. Melt butter in a medium saucepan. Add flour and stir for 2 minutes. Remove from heat. Gradually add milk, stirring constantly. Return pan to heat, stirring continuously until sauce thickens and comes to the boil. Remove from heat. Stir in cheese, cayenne pepper and nutmeg. Season. Cool slightly. Stir in spinach. Add egg yolks one at a time, beating well. Using an electric mixer, beat egg whites to a stiff foam. Carefully fold half the egg whites into the sauce. Carefully fold sauce mixture into remaining egg whites. Spoon mixture into prepared dish to three-quarters full. Place into a heatproof dish. Pour hot water into the outer dish to come within 3 cm of the top of the soufflé. Bake at 180°C for 40–45 minutes or until risen and golden. For individual soufflés, bake for 30–35 minutes. *Serves 3–4 as a light meal.*

# BEEF CASSEROLE

1 kg chuck or blade steak
¼ cup Champion standard grade flour
2 tablespoons oil
1 large onion, chopped
3 cups beef stock
2 carrots, sliced
salt and freshly ground black pepper

1 bay leaf
sprig of thyme
sprig of parsley
1 tablespoon Edmonds Fielder's
   cornflour
1 tablespoon water

Trim fat from meat and cut into 2.5 cm cubes. Heat oil in a heavy-based frying pan. Add onion and cook for 5 minutes until soft. Using a slotted spoon, remove onion and place in a casserole dish. Coat meat in flour. Add one quarter of meat and quickly brown on all sides. Remove from pan. Repeat with remaining meat, one-quarter at a time. Place meat in dish with onions. Gradually add stock to saucepan, stirring. Bring to the boil. Add carrots. Season with salt and pepper. Make a bouquet garni with bay leaf, thyme and parsley. Add bouquet garni and liquid to casserole dish. Cover and cook at 160°C for 1¼ hours or until meat is tender. Remove bouquet garni. Mix cornflour to a paste with water. Stir into casserole then return to the oven for a further 15 minutes. Serve with mashed potatoes and seasonal vegetables of your choice. *Serves 6–8.*

### BEEF AND MUSHROOM CASSEROLE
Replace half the beef stock with *red wine*. Add *¼ cup tomato purée* and *1 cup sliced mushrooms*.

### BEEF AND MUSTARD CASSEROLE
At end of cooking time, stir in *1 tablespoon wholegrain mustard*.

### BEEF AND PEPPER CASSEROLE
Add *1 chopped red or green capsicum* when cooking the onions.

# BEEF WELLINGTON

1.25 kg fillet of beef
freshly ground black pepper
2 tablespoons oil
250 g green peppercorn pâté
100 g button mushrooms, sliced

400 g chilled puff pastry
  (or pre-rolled pastry)
1 egg yolk
1 tablespoon water

Trim fat from meat. Wrap string around the fillet to maintain the shape. Season all over with pepper. Heat oil in a heavy-based frying pan. To seal in juices, cook meat over a high heat until evenly browned. Transfer to a large roasting dish. Bake at 180°C for 10 minutes. Remove from oven and allow meat to cool completely. Remove string and discard. Beat pâté with a wooden spoon until smooth. Spread pâté over entire surface of meat. Press mushrooms into the pâté on top of the meat. Roll pastry into a rectangle approximately 25 x 35 cm. (The exact size required will depend on the size of the meat.) Place meat top-side down in the centre of the pastry. Trim pastry, allowing enough just to encase the meat with a small overlap. Whisk together egg yolk and water. Fold ends and edge of pastry over meat, brushing with egg mixture to seal. Place sealed-edge down in a baking dish. Brush all over with egg mixture. Decorate with pastry offcuts and brush these with egg mixture. Bake at 220°C for 5 minutes. Reduce heat to 180°C and cook for a further 35 minutes for medium-rare or 40 minutes for medium. Stand meat for 10 minutes before slicing. If desired, serve with gravy, or Green Peppercorn Sauce (see page 182). *Serves 4–6.*

# BONED PORK LOIN WITH SPINACH AND PRUNE STUFFING

150 g spinach, trimmed
1 tablespoon water
½ cup chopped pitted prunes
1 small Granny Smith apple, grated
¼ cup chopped pistachio nuts
1.5 kg boned pork loin
salt (preferably sea salt)
cranberry sauce or jelly, to serve

Place spinach and water in a saucepan. Cover and cook over a medium heat just until spinach wilts. Drain in a sieve. Refresh under cold running water. Squeeze out excess liquid. Combine prunes, apple and nuts in a bowl. Lay pork loin rind-side down on a flat surface. Lay spinach leaves out flat over the surface of the meat. Spread prune mixture over top. Roll meat up. Secure at intervals with string. Place join-down in a roasting dish. Score rind with a sharp knife. Rub in a little salt. Bake at 200°C for 10 minutes, then reduce heat to 160°C and cook for 1½–2 hours. Meat is cooked when juices run clear. Cover with foil and stand for 10 minutes before carving. Serve with cranberry sauce or jelly. *Serves 4–6.*

# BRAISED LAMB KNUCKLES IN A RICH GRAVY

½ cup Champion standard grade flour
salt and freshly ground black pepper
8 lamb knuckles
2 tablespoons oil
1 onion, finely chopped
1 teaspoon crushed garlic
1½ cups red wine
¼ cup tomato purée

2 cups beef stock
1 tablespoon Edmonds Fielder's
  cornflour
1 tablespoon water
salt and freshly ground black pepper
3 sprigs rosemary
sprigs of rosemary to garnish

Season flour with salt and pepper. Place in a shallow dish. Trim excess fat from knuckles. Roll in the flour mixture to coat. Heat oil in a large, heavy-based frying pan. Cook 4 knuckles at a time, turning occasionally, until browned. Transfer to a roasting pan. Repeat with remaining knuckles. Cover roasting dish and bake at 150°C for 1 hour. Remove dish from oven and pour off excess fat. While knuckles are cooking, add onion to the frying pan and cook for 5 minutes until soft. Add garlic, wine, tomato purée and stock. Mix cornflour to a paste with water. Add to pan, stirring constantly until sauce thickens slightly and comes to the boil. Season. Pour over knuckles. Lay rosemary on top. Cover dish tightly with foil. Bake at 150°C for 2 hours, turning knuckles occasionally. Serve with mashed potato or a combination of mashed potato and mashed kumara. Garnish with sprigs of rosemary. *Serves 4.*

# PEPPERED EYE-FILLET STEAKS
# WITH BÉARNAISE SAUCE

*4 eye-fillet steaks (about 2–2.5 cm thick)*
*freshly ground black pepper*

*a little oil to cook*
*Béarnaise Sauce (see page 182)*

Roll steaks in pepper to lightly coat. Pour sufficient oil into a heavy-based frying pan just to cover the base. Heat pan. Cook steaks over a high heat for 3–4 minutes on each side for rare, for 1–2 minutes longer on each side for medium, and a little longer for well done. Serve with Béarnaise Sauce and vegetables or salad of your choice. *Serves 4.*

# RACK OF LAMB WITH A ROSEMARY CRUST

½ cup dry breadcrumbs
2 tablespoons finely chopped rosemary
2 cloves garlic, crushed
salt and freshly ground black
   pepper to season

¼ cup melted butter
2 racks lamb, each with 6 cutlets

Combine breadcrumbs, rosemary, garlic, salt, pepper and butter in a bowl. Mix well. Trim any excess fat from lamb racks. Spread crumb mixture over the fatty surface of the lamb racks, pressing firmly. Place lamb racks, crust-side up, in a roasting dish. Bake at 200°C for 25–30 minutes or until the meat is cooked to the desired level. Cover with foil and stand for 10 minutes before slicing into cutlets. *Serves 4.*

# QUICK APPLE AND BERRY CRUMBLE

2 x 567 g cans apple slices
   *in natural juice*
200 g blueberries (fresh or frozen)
¼ cup caster sugar

TOPPING

100 g butter
½ cup brown sugar
2½ cups Fleming's rolled oats

Drain any juice from the apples. Spread apple evenly over the base of an ovenproof dish. Scatter berries over top. Sprinkle over sugar. To make the topping, place butter and brown sugar in a saucepan. Stir over a heat until butter melts. Add rolled oats, mixing until thoroughly coated with butter mixture. Spoon crumble topping over fruit. Press down lightly with a fork. Bake at 180°C for 30 minutes until topping is golden and the fruit is beginning to bubble. ***Serves 6.*** *(Top right)*

## VARIATION

Add ½ **cup chopped nuts** or **coconut** to the topping mixture. Other berries can be used as an alternative to blueberries.

# INDIVIDUAL PAVLOVAS

4 egg whites
1½ cups caster sugar
1 teaspoon DYC white vinegar
1 teaspoon vanilla essence
1 tablespoon Edmonds Fielder's
   cornflour

whipped cream
fresh berries and grated
   chocolate to garnish

Preheat oven to 180°C. Using an electric mixer, beat egg whites and caster sugar for 10–15 minutes or until thick and glossy. Mix vinegar, essence and cornflour together. Add to meringue. Beat on high speed for a further 5 minutes. Line a baking tray with baking paper. Draw four 12-cm-diameter circles on the paper. Spread meringue to within 1 cm of the edge of the circles, keeping the shapes as round and even as possible. Place tray in preheated oven, then turn oven down to 100°C. Bake for 50 minutes. Turn off oven. Open door slightly and leave pavlovas until cold. Carefully lift pavlovas onto individual plates. Decorate with whipped cream, berries and grated chocolate. ***Serves 4.*** *(Middle right)*

# RICE PUDDING

5 tablespoons short grain rice
2 tablespoons sugar
¾ cup sultanas (optional)
3 cups milk

2–3 drops vanilla essence
1 teaspoon butter
¼ teaspoon ground nutmeg
drained canned apricot halves, to serve

Place rice, sugar and sultanas in the bottom of an ovenproof dish. Add milk and essence. Mix well. Add butter. Sprinkle nutmeg over surface. Cover and bake at 150°C for 2 hours, stirring two to three times in first hour. This pudding should be creamy when cooked. Serve with apricot halves. ***Serves 4.*** *(Below left)*

# SPONGE ROLL

3 eggs
pinch of salt
½ cup caster sugar
½ teaspoon vanilla essence
5 tablespoons Champion standard
   grade flour

1 teaspoon Edmonds baking powder
25 g butter, melted
caster or icing sugar
jam or honey to spread

whipped cream

Using an electric mixer, beat eggs and salt for 2 minutes. Add sugar and essence and beat until thick and pale. Sift flour and baking powder together. Fold lightly into egg mixture. Fold in butter. Pour into a greased 20 x 30 cm sponge roll tin. Bake at 200°C for 8–10 minutes or until golden and cake springs back when lightly touched. Turn out onto a cloth or greaseproof paper sprinkled with caster or icing sugar. Trim edges. Roll into a log, including the cloth or paper in the roll and working from the short side. Set aside until cold. Carefully unroll log. Spread with jam or honey, then whipped cream. Again roll from the short side but do not include the cloth or paper this time. To serve, cut into slices using a sharp knife. *(Below left)*

# STEAMED CHOCOLATE PUDDINGS

2 cups Champion standard grade flour
1 teaspoon Edmonds baking powder
¼ cup cocoa
125 g butter, cut into cubes
100 g dark chocolate, chopped
¾ cup caster sugar

1 teaspoon vanilla essence
1 teaspoon Edmonds baking soda
1 cup milk, warmed
2 eggs, lightly beaten
butter for greasing
custard or cream to serve

Sift flour, baking powder and cocoa into a bowl. Combine butter, chocolate, sugar and essence in the top of a double boiler or in a heatproof bowl. Sit over simmering water. Stir constantly until butter and chocolate melt and mixture is smooth. Dissolve baking soda in milk. Fold butter mixture, milk and eggs into dry ingredients. Do not overmix. Thoroughly grease 6 ovenproof teacups or 1-cup-capacity ramekins with butter. Divide mixture evenly between prepared cups. Place cups in a roasting pan. Fill pan with hot water to halfway up the sides of the cups. Cover dish with a sheet of greaseproof paper, then a sheet of foil, securing the edges to seal in steam. Bake at 200°C for 45 minutes. Stand for 5 minutes before carefully removing the covers. Invert puddings onto warm serving plates. Serve with custard or cream. **Serves 6.** *(Above right)*

# CHOCOLATE CHIP BISCUITS

125 g butter, softened
¼ cup sugar
3 tablespoons sweetened condensed milk
few drops vanilla essence

1½ cups Champion standard
   grade flour
1 teaspoon Edmonds baking powder
½ cup chocolate chips

Cream butter, sugar, condensed milk and essence until light and fluffy. Sift flour and baking powder together. Mix sifted dry ingredients and chocolate chips into creamed mixture. Roll tablespoons of mixture into balls. Place on a greased oven tray and flatten with a floured fork. Bake at 180°C for 20 minutes. *Makes 25.*

# BARBECUE MENU

# BACON-WRAPPED SAUSAGES

*8 quality sausages*
*8 rashers rindless bacon*

*wholegrain mustard, to spread*

Prick each sausage with a fork. Lay bacon on a flat surface. Spread each rasher with a little mustard. Wrap a rasher around each sausage. Cook on a preheated barbecue for 12–15 minutes until cooked through, turning occasionally. *(Top left)*

# BARBECUED VEGETABLES

*½ cup olive oil*
*1 teaspoon crushed garlic*
*4 capsicums, any colour*
*4 small courgettes*

*1 small eggplant*
*2 red onions*
*8 flat mushrooms*

Combine oil and garlic. Prepare vegetables. Halve capsicums, remove core and seeds. Cut each half into 3 pieces. Trim courgettes. Cut in half lengthwise. Trim ends off eggplant. Cut into 1-cm-thick rounds. Peel onions. Cut into quarters. Brush vegetables liberally all over with the oil. Cook on a preheated barbecue until tender. Serve with Sundried Tomato Pesto (see page 177). *(Below right)*

# GARLIC AND SWEET CHILLI PRAWNS

*2 tablespoons lemon juice*
*2 tablespoons sweet chilli sauce*
*2 tablespoons chopped coriander*
*1 tablespoon olive oil*

*2 cloves garlic, crushed*
*24 uncooked king prawns*
*lemon wedges to garnish*

Combine lemon juice, chilli sauce, coriander, oil and garlic in a medium bowl. Add prawns and mix well. Cover and refrigerate for 2 hours. Cook on a preheated barbecue for 4–5 minutes until cooked through, turning once. Transfer to a serving plate. Garnish with lemon wedges. *(Middle left)*

# HONEY AND THYME MARINATED CHICKEN BREASTS

*2 tablespoons DYC white vinegar*
*2 tablespoons olive oil*
*2 tablespoons soy sauce*
*2 tablespoons honey*
*2 tablespoons tomato purée*

*2 cloves garlic, crushed*
*2 teaspoons finely chopped thyme*
*4 single boneless skinless chicken breasts*
  *(or chicken portions)*

Combine all ingredients except chicken. Mix well. Place chicken breasts between 2 sheets of plastic wrap. Using a heavy object, pound to an even thickness of about 1 cm. Place in a single layer in a glass or ceramic dish. Pour over marinade and turn to coat. Leave to marinate in the refrigerator for at least 1 hour. Cook over a medium heat on a preheated barbecue for 8–10 minutes until cooked through, turning once. **Serves 4.** *(Top right)*

# PRESERVES

## APPLE AND PASSIONFRUIT JELLY

2 kg cooking apples, e.g. Granny Smiths
1 cup passionfruit pulp
  (about 12 passionfruit)

2 tablespoons coarsely grated lemon zest
water
sugar

Peel, quarter and core apples. Cut each quarter into 4 pieces. Place apple, passionfruit pulp and lemon zest in a saucepan. Add sufficient water to just cover the fruit. Cover pan and bring to the boil. Reduce heat and simmer for 1 hour until apple is soft and pulpy. Strain mixture through a jelly bag. (Alternatively, to strain through muslin, place 3 layers of muslin over a large bowl, allowing a little slack for the weight of the fruit. Tie in place with string. Slowly tip apple from the saucepan onto the muslin cloth.) Leave to sit for 6 hours. Do not disturb this process or the jelly will turn cloudy. Measure the quantity of juice. For every cup of juice, add 1 cup of sugar. Combine juice and sugar in a saucepan. Bring to the boil. Boil vigorously for about 30 minutes or until setting point is reached. To test for setting point, drop a little jelly onto a saucer. If a skin forms as it cools, the jelly will set. On a sugar thermometer the setting point is reached at 105°C. Use a paper towel to quickly skim any scum off the surface of the jelly. Working quickly, ladle jelly into sterilised jars. Top with cellophane jam covers and secure with a rubber band. Leave jelly to set — do not move jars until they are cold. Store in a cool, dark place. This jelly will keep for up to 1 year. **Makes about 3 cups.** (Top)

## APRICOT CURD

250 g fresh ripe apricots
2 tablespoons water
¾ cup sugar
50 g butter, chopped

finely grated zest of 1 lemon
juice of 1 lemon
3 egg yolks, lightly beaten

Cut apricots in half. Remove stones. Combine apricots and water in a saucepan. Bring to the boil over a medium heat. Simmer for about 4 minutes until pulpy, stirring frequently. Tip into a sieve, then rub pulp through the sieve. Combine pulp, sugar, butter, lemon zest and juice in a double boiler or heatproof bowl. Sit it over a saucepan of simmering water. Stir until sugar has dissolved and butter has melted. Add yolks, stirring constantly until the mixture thickens. Pour into clean, sterilised jars. Seal. Cool, then refrigerate. Stored in the refrigerator, Apricot Curd will keep for up to 1 month. **Makes about 2 cups.** (Middle and below left)

## REFRIGERATED FIG AND ORANGE JAM

1 kg ready soaked dried figs
finely grated zest of 2 oranges
1 cup freshly squeezed orange juice

1 litre water
2 cups sugar

Cut each fig into 6 pieces. Combine figs, orange zest and juice and water in a large saucepan. Bring to the boil. Simmer for 30 minutes until figs are tender. Add sugar, stirring until dissolved. Simmer for 45 minutes or until mixture is thick, stirring frequently to prevent burning. Remove from heat and allow to cool, uncovered, in the saucepan. Transfer to covered containers and refrigerate. Stored in the refrigerator, this jam will keep for up to 3 months. **Makes about 3½ cups.**

  N.B. For a chunkier jam, cut figs into quarters. (Below right)

# REFRIGERATED ORANGE, LIME AND GINGER MARMALADE

*1 litre freshly squeezed orange juice*
*finely sliced zest of 2 oranges*
*juice of 6 limes*

*2½ cups sugar*
*½ cup chopped crystallised ginger*

Combine orange juice, orange zest and lime juice in a large saucepan. Cover pan and bring to the boil. Simmer for 1 hour. Add sugar. Boil uncovered for 30 minutes. Remove from heat. Add ginger. Cool. Transfer to clean jars or containers. Covered and refrigerated, this marmalade will keep for up to 3 months. *Makes 4 cups.*

# DRIED FRUIT COMPOTE

2 cups freshly squeezed orange juice
    (about 8 oranges)
½ cup water
⅓ cup liquid honey
2 cinnamon sticks

⅓ cup brandy
200 g dried apricots
150 g dried figs
100 g pitted prunes

Strain orange juice through a fine sieve into a saucepan. Add water, honey and one cinnamon stick. Stir over a low heat until honey dissolves. Bring to the boil, reduce heat and simmer for 45 minutes. Remove cinnamon stick and discard. Stir in brandy. Pack dried fruit and remaining cinnamon stick into a clean sterilised jar. Pour syrup over fruit. Cover jar tightly with a lid. Cool. Store in the refrigerator. Serve with whipped cream, ice-cream or yoghurt.

# PEACH CONSERVE

2 cups sugar
1/2 cup water
1/4 cup freshly squeezed lemon juice

1 kg firm, ripe peaches,
    peeled, stoned and sliced

Place sugar and water in a saucepan. Stir over a low heat until sugar has dissolved. Bring to the boil, stirring constantly. Reduce heat, add lemon juice and peaches and simmer for 5 minutes. Remove from heat and set aside for 1 hour. Reheat peaches. Bring to the boil. Reduce heat and simmer for 30 minutes until peaches are translucent and the syrup is thick. Spoon into a hot, sterilised 750 ml jar. Cover with a lid. Refrigerated, this conserve will keep for up to 3 months. **Makes 3 cups.** *(Below left)*
    N.B. This conserve is not as thick as jam.

# PEACHES IN SPICED BRANDY

1 litre water
3 tablespoons lemon juice
12 medium firm, ripe peaches
2 1/2 cups water

1 kg sugar
1 cinnamon stick
4 whole cloves
3/4 cup brandy

Bring first measure of water and lemon juice to the boil in a saucepan. Cut peaches in half. Add peaches 4 at a time and cook for 1 1/2 minutes or until liquid returns to the boil. Using a slotted spoon, transfer peaches to iced water to cool. Remove skins and stones. Combine second measure of water and the sugar in a large saucepan. Bring to the boil. Carefully add 12 peach halves to the syrup, return to the boil, then reduce heat and simmer gently for 2 minutes. Using a slotted spoon, remove peaches and set aside to cool. Repeat with remaining peaches. Add cinnamon stick and cloves to the syrup. Return syrup to the boil. Boil vigorously for 20 minutes or until it reaches 105°C on a sugar thermometer. Remove cinnamon stick and cloves. Stir in brandy. Pack peaches into 2 clean, sterilised 1 litre jars. Pour syrup over peaches until overflowing the jar. (Peaches must be completely covered with syrup.) Seal. Stored in a cool place, these peaches will keep for up to 1 year. *(Above right)*

# CHARGRILLED CAPSICUMS WITH GARLIC AND ROSEMARY

6 capsicums, any colour
¼ cup olive oil
1 clove garlic, crushed

2 teaspoons rosemary leaves
freshly ground black pepper

Preheat oven grill. Place capsicums in a baking dish. Place about 10 cm from heat source and grill until skins blacken slightly and blister, turning occasionally. Remove from oven and cover with a baking tray until cool. Core, seed and peel capsicums. Cut into 1-cm-wide strips. Place in a bowl. Combine oil, garlic and rosemary. Pour over capsicums and toss lightly to combine. Season with pepper. Covered and refrigerated, these chargrilled capsicums will keep for 3–4 days.

N.B. Chargrilled capsicums are a delicious addition to summer salads, sandwiches, pizzas or as part of an antipasto platter.

## VARIATION

For Chargrilled Capsicums with Chilli, substitute ½ teaspoon finely chopped red chilli for the garlic and rosemary.

# HONEY AND BEER MUSTARD

*¹/₂ cup white mustard seeds*
*2 tablespoons black mustard seeds*
*¹/₂ cup DYC cider vinegar*

*¹/₂ cup beer*
*1 teaspoon salt*
*¹/₄ cup liquid honey*

Combine mustard seeds, vinegar and beer in a small bowl. Cover and set aside for 6–8 hours or overnight. Place in a food processor with salt and honey. Blend to desired consistency — for a smoother mustard, blend for a longer time. Pour into sterilised jars. Cover with a lid. The mustard will thicken with standing. This mustard will keep for up to 6 months. *Makes 2 cups.*
*(Top left and right)*

# WHITE WINE AND ROSEMARY MUSTARD

*¹/₂ cup white mustard seeds*
*2 tablespoons black mustard seeds*
*¹/₂ cup DYC white wine vinegar*
*¹/₂ cup dry white wine*

*2 tablespoons chopped rosemary leaves*
*1 teaspoon salt*
*¹/₄ cup sugar*

Combine mustard seeds, vinegar and wine in a small bowl. Cover and set aside for 6–8 hours or overnight. Place in a food processor with rosemary, salt and sugar. Blend to desired consistency — for a smoother mustard, blend for a longer time. Pour into sterilised jars. Cover with a lid. The mustard will thicken with standing. This mustard will keep for up to 1 month. *Makes 1¹/₂ cups.*
N.B. The addition of rosemary reduces the shelf life. *(Centre)*

# MARINATED OLIVES WITH HERBS

*500 g Kalamata olives*
*2 cloves garlic, peeled*
*2 bay leaves*
*3 sprigs rosemary*

*1 teaspoon black peppercorns*
*300 ml olive oil*
*⅓ cup DYC white wine vinegar*

Place olives in a sieve and drain thoroughly. Cut garlic cloves in half lengthwise. Rinse bay leaves and rosemary under cold running water. Pat dry with paper towels. Pack olives into a clean, sterilised 750-ml jar, adding garlic, bay leaves, rosemary and peppercorns as you go. Combine oil and vinegar in a saucepan. Heat until warm. Pour over olives — the olives must be completely covered with the mixture. Seal jar. Store in a cool, dark place for 2–3 weeks before using. Marinated olives will keep for up to 3 months.

## VARIATION

For Marinated Olives with Chilli, substitute **1 small red chilli**, which has been seeded and thinly sliced, for the herbs.

# OVEN-DRIED TOMATOES

*acid-free or low-acid tomatoes*
*olive oil to cover*

Preheat oven to 110°C. Cut tomatoes in half lengthwise. Arrange in a single layer, cut-side down, on a wire rack. Place rack over a shallow baking tray that has been lined with foil. Place tray in oven, leaving the door slightly ajar. Cook for 7–9 hours (see note below), turning the tomatoes halfway through the cooking time. Pack tomatoes in a sterilised jar. Pour in sufficient olive oil to completely cover the tomatoes. Cover jar with a lid. Refrigerated, oven-dried tomatoes will keep for up to 1 month.

N.B. For semi-dried tomatoes, the cooking time will be about 7 hours. For fully dried tomatoes, the cooking time will be about 9 hours. These times are only estimates, as the size of the tomatoes will influence the cooking time. The oil may appear to solidify slightly when the jars of tomatoes are refrigerated. Remove from the refrigerator and allow to return to room temperature before using.

# OLIVE TAPENADE

*4 anchovy fillets*
*200 g pitted black olives*
  *(preferably Kalamata olives)*
*2 tablespoons capers, drained*
*2 cloves garlic, crushed*

*1 tablespoon lemon juice*
*1 teaspoon oregano leaves*
*½ cup olive oil*
*freshly ground black pepper*

Rinse anchovy fillets under cold running water. Pat dry with a paper towel. Put anchovy fillets, olives, capers, garlic, lemon juice and oregano in a food processor. Gradually add oil, pulsing until the mixture forms a coarse paste. Season with pepper. Covered and refrigerated, tapenade will keep for up to 1 week. ***Makes 1¼ cups.*** *(Middle right)*

# ROASTED RED CAPSICUM AND CORIANDER PESTO

*2 red capsicums, roasted (see page 188*
  *for method), peeled and seeded*
*1 cup lightly packed coriander leaves*
*2 cloves garlic, crushed*

*¼ cup toasted pinenuts*
  *(see Pesto page 182 for method)*
*1 tablespoon olive oil*
*salt and freshly ground black pepper*

Roughly chop capsicums. Place in a food processor with coriander, garlic, pinenuts and oil. Pulse until the mixture forms a coarse paste. Season with salt and pepper. Covered and refrigerated, this pesto will keep for 2–3 days. ***Makes 1 cup.*** *(Below right)*

# SUNDRIED TOMATO PESTO

*1 cup drained sundried tomatoes in oil*
*2 cloves garlic, crushed*
*¼ cup toasted pinenuts*
  *(see Pesto page 182 for method)*

*¼ cup finely grated parmesan cheese*
*about ½ cup olive oil*
*salt and freshly ground black pepper*

Place sundried tomatoes, garlic, pinenuts and parmesan in a food processor. Gradually add oil, pulsing until the mixture forms a coarse paste. Season with salt and pepper. Covered and refrigerated, this pesto will keep for up to 1 week. ***Makes 1½ cups.*** *(Above right)*

# WALNUT PESTO

*2 cups (225 g) quality walnut pieces*
*½ cup loosely packed parsley sprigs*
*½ cup finely grated parmesan cheese*

*2 cloves garlic, crushed*
*½ cup olive oil*
*salt and freshly ground black pepper*

Place walnuts, parsley, parmesan and garlic in a food processor. Gradually add oil, pulsing until the mixture forms a coarse paste. Season with salt and pepper. Covered and refrigerated, this pesto will keep for up to 1 week. ***Makes about 1½ cups.*** *(Below left)*

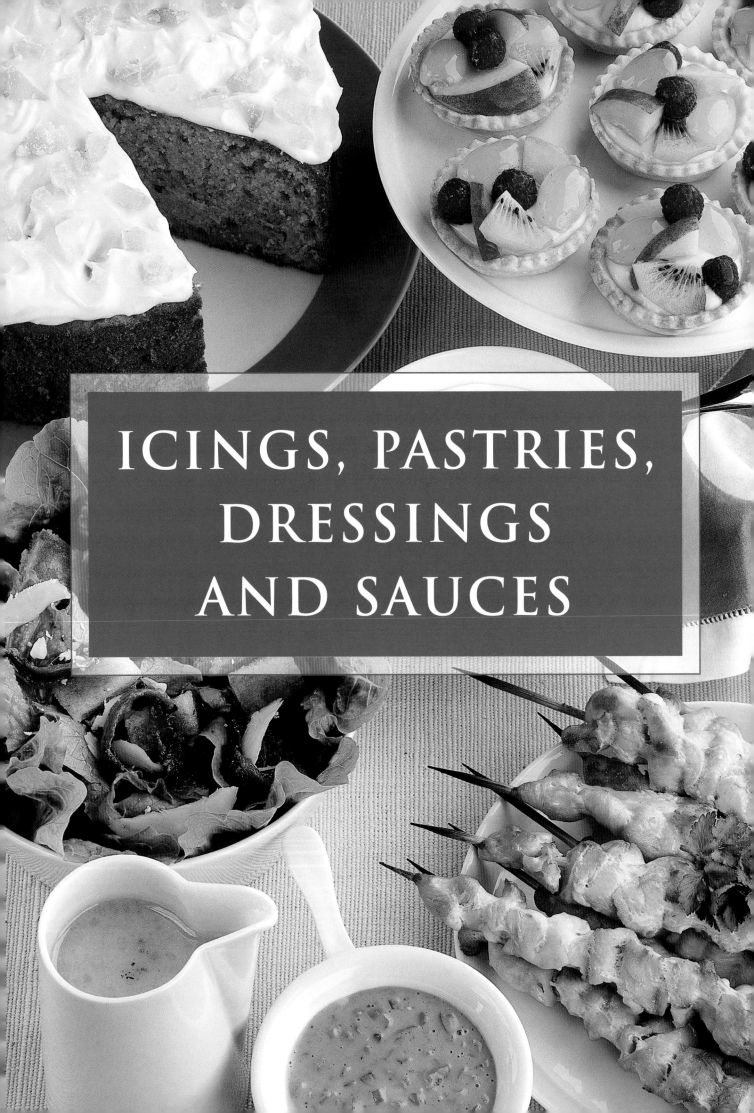

# ICINGS, PASTRIES, DRESSINGS AND SAUCES

## BUTTER ICING

*100 g butter, softened*
*¼ teaspoon vanilla essence*
*2 cups icing sugar, sifted*
*1–2 tablespoons hot water*

Cream butter until light and fluffy. Add essence. Gradually beat in icing sugar, beating until smooth. Add sufficient water to give a spreading consistency.

## CHOCOLATE BUTTER ICING

Sift 2 tablespoons cocoa with the icing sugar in above recipe.

## WHITE ICING

*2 cups icing sugar*
*¼ teaspoon butter, softened*
*2 tablespoons water, approximately*
*¼ teaspoon vanilla essence*

Sift icing sugar into a bowl. Add butter. Add sufficient water to mix to a spreadable consistency. Flavour with essence.

## CHOCOLATE ICING

Sift *1 tablespoon cocoa* with the icing sugar in the above recipe.

## COFFEE ICING

Dissolve *2 teaspoons instant coffee powder* in *1 tablespoon hot water*. Mix into icing sugar and proceed as for White Icing recipe above.

## LEMON ICING

In the recipe for White Icing above, replace essence with *1 teaspoon grated lemon zest*. Replace water with *lemon juice*. Add a few drops of *yellow food colouring* if wished.

## ORANGE ICING

In the recipe for White Icing above, replace essence with *2 teaspoons grated orange zest*. Replace water with *orange juice*. Add a few drops of *yellow and red food colouring* if wished.

## MELTED CHOCOLATE ICING (GANACHE)

*200 g cooking chocolate*
*  or dark chocolate*
*25 g butter*
*½ cup cream*

Break chocolate into top of a double boiler or a small heatproof bowl. Sit over simmering water. Add butter and cream. Stir constantly until melted and mixture is smooth. Set aside until cool. Beat until thick before using.

## CREAM CHEESE ICING

*2 tablespoons butter, softened*
*¼ cup cream cheese*
*1 cup icing sugar*
*½ teaspoon grated lemon zest*

Beat butter and cream cheese until creamy. Mix in icing sugar and lemon zest, beating well to combine.

## LEMON CURD

*50 g butter*
*¾ cup sugar*
*1 cup lemon juice*
*2 eggs, beaten*
*1 teaspoon finely grated lemon zest*

Melt the butter in the top of a double boiler. Stir in sugar and lemon juice until sugar is dissolved. Add eggs and lemon zest. Place over boiling water and cook, stirring all the time until mixture thickens. Cool. Store in the refrigerator in a covered container. *Makes 2 cups.*

## FLAKY PASTRY

*2 cups Champion high grade flour*
*¼ teaspoon salt*
*200 g butter*
*6 tablespoons cold water,*
*  approximately*

Sift flour and salt into a bowl. Cut one-quarter of the butter into the flour until it resembles fine breadcrumbs. Add sufficient water to mix to a stiff dough. On a lightly floured board roll out dough to a rectangle 0.5–1 cm thick. With the short end of the rectangle facing you, dot two-thirds of the pastry with a third of the remaining butter to within 1 cm of the dough edge. Fold the unbuttered pastry into the middle of the pastry. Fold the buttered section over to the folded edge. Seal the edges with a rolling pin and mark the dough with the rolling pin to form corrugations. Give the pastry a quarter turn. Roll into a rectangle. Repeat twice until all the butter is used. Chill pastry for 5 minutes between rollings if possible. Use as required for savoury pies and vol au vents. *Makes 500 g.*

## PUFF PASTRY

In the Flaky Pastry recipe above increase **butter to 250 g**. Roll and fold the pastry 6 times.

## SHORT PASTRY

*2 cups Champion standard grade flour*
*¼ teaspoon salt*
*125 g butter*
*cold water*

Sift flour and salt together. Cut in the butter until it resembles fine breadcrumbs. Mix to a stiff dough with a little water. Roll out very lightly and do not handle more than is necessary. Use as required for sweet or savoury pies and tarts, and quiches. *Makes 375 g.*

## WHOLEMEAL PASTRY

In the recipe for Short Pastry, replace flour with *Champion wholemeal flour* and add *1 teaspoon Edmonds baking powder*.

## FOOD-PROCESSOR SHORT PASTRY

Use ingredients listed for Short Pastry. Have butter and water very cold. Dice butter. Put flour in food processor. Add butter. Pulse until it resembles fine breadcrumbs. Add water by drops and pulse until mixture forms small balls. Do not overmix. Turn out onto a lightly floured surface. Knead lightly. Wrap and chill for at least 15 minutes, before rolling.

## SWEET SHORTCRUST PASTRY

*1 cup Champion standard grade flour*
*75 g butter*
*¼ cup sugar*
*1 egg yolk*
*1 tablespoon water*

Sift flour. Cut in butter until it resembles fine breadcrumbs. Stir in sugar. Add egg yolk and water. Mix to a stiff dough. Chill for 30 minutes before using. Use as required for sweet pies and tarts. *Makes about 200 g.* (This pastry can be made in a food processor.)

## NUT PASTRY

To the Sweet Shortcrust Pastry recipe above, *add ½ cup chopped walnuts or nuts of your choice* before mixing to a stiff dough.

## SPICE PASTRY

To the flour in the Sweet Shortcrust Pastry recipe above, add *2 teaspoons mixed spice.*

## AVOCADO DRESSING

*1 ripe avocado, peeled*
*    and roughly chopped*
*juice of 1 lemon or lime*
*¼ cup oil*
*½ teaspoon sugar*
*few drops of Tabasco sauce*
*salt and freshly ground black*
*    pepper to season*

Put avocado into food processor or blender. Process until smooth. Add lime juice, oil and sugar. Process to combine. Season to taste with Tabasco, salt and pepper. *Makes ½ cup.*

## BLUE CHEESE DRESSING

*100 g blue vein cheese*
*1 cup (250 g) sour cream*
*    (or ¾ cup cream and*
*    ¼ cup DYC white vinegar)*
*1 clove garlic, crushed*
*2 to 3 tablespoons milk*

Mash cheese with fork. Add sour cream, garlic and milk. Beat or blend until smooth. *Makes 1½ cups.*

## CAESAR SALAD DRESSING

*1 egg*
*1 anchovy, drained and*
*   roughly chopped*
*2 teaspoons DYC white vinegar*
*1 teaspoon lemon juice*
*1 small clove garlic, crushed*
*¼ cup olive oil*
*freshly ground black pepper*

Cook egg in boiling water for 1 minute. Drain. Break open egg and tip into a small bowl. Add anchovy, vinegar, lemon juice and garlic. Whisk vigorously to combine. Add oil in a continuous stream, whisking constantly. Season to taste with pepper.

## FRENCH DRESSING (VINAIGRETTE)

*³/4 cup oil*
*¼ cup DYC white, wine or cider*
*   vinegar, or lemon juice*
*¼ teaspoon dry mustard*
*salt and freshly ground black*
*   pepper to season*
*1 clove garlic, crushed*
*1 tablespoon chopped parsley,*
*   chives or fresh basil*

Put all ingredients into a screw-top jar. Shake well to combine. *Makes 1 cup.*

## MUSTARD DRESSING

Add **2 teaspoons wholegrain mustard** to the French Dressing above.

## MAYONNAISE

*1 egg yolk*
*½ teaspoon salt*
*¼ teaspoon dry mustard*
*pinch of cayenne pepper*
*1 tablespoon DYC malt vinegar,*
*   or lemon juice*
*1 cup oil*

Mix egg yolk, salt, mustard and cayenne pepper in a bowl. Add vinegar. Very gradually add oil, beating constantly with a whisk or beater. As mixture begins to combine add remaining oil in a fine stream while beating. If mixture is too thick, add more vinegar. *Makes 1 cup.*

## QUICK BLENDER MAYONNAISE

*2 eggs*
*1 tablespoon DYC white or*
*   wine vinegar, or lemon juice*
*½ teaspoon dry mustard*
*½ teaspoon salt*
*pinch of cayenne pepper*
*1 cup oil*

Put eggs, vinegar, mustard, salt and cayenne pepper into food processor or blender and process until combined. Continue blending while adding oil in a thin, steady stream, blending until thick. If too thick, add extra vinegar. *Makes 1¼ cups.*

## UNCOOKED (CONDENSED MILK) SALAD DRESSING

*397 g can sweetened condensed milk*
*1 cup DYC malt vinegar*
*1 teaspoon salt*
*2 teaspoons dry mustard*

Stir all ingredients until combined. Leave to stand for a few minutes to thicken before using. *Makes about 2 cups.*

## YOGHURT DRESSING

*1 cup natural unsweetened yoghurt*
*1 tablespoon lemon juice*
*¼ teaspoon dry mustard*
*salt and freshly ground black*
*   pepper to season*

Stir all ingredients until combined. Chill before using. *Makes 1 cup.*

## APPLE SAUCE

*3 to 4 large cooking apples,*
*   peeled and chopped*
*1 tablespoon water*
*1 tablespoon butter*
*2 cloves or few drops lemon juice*
*sugar*

Put apples, water, butter and cloves into a saucepan. Simmer until apples are pulped. Blend or beat with a fork until smooth. Add sugar to taste. *Makes about 1½ cups.*

## BÉARNAISE SAUCE

*3 tablespoons DYC wine vinegar*
*  or tarragon vinegar*
*6 peppercorns*
*1 bay leaf*
*¼ small onion, chopped*
*2 egg yolks*
*75–100 g butter*
*salt and freshly ground black pepper*
*1 tablespoon chopped parsley*

Put vinegar, peppercorns, bay leaf and onion into a small saucepan. Bring to the boil and reduce to 1 tablespoon. Strain and reserve liquid. Place yolks and reserved liquid in a double boiler and lightly beat. Gradually add butter in small pieces beating until sauce is thick enough to show the marks of whisk. Do not allow to boil or sauce will curdle. Season to taste with salt and pepper. Add parsley. Keep warm. *Makes about ³⁄4 cup.*

## CUCUMBER AND MINT RAITA

*³⁄4 cup natural unsweetened yoghurt*
*½ cup grated telegraph cucumber*
*1 tablespoon chopped mint*
*salt and freshly ground black*
*  pepper to season*

Combine all ingredients in a bowl. Mix well.

## GREEN PEPPERCORN SAUCE

*50 g butter*
*2 tablespoons lemon juice*
*2 tablespoons green peppercorns, rinsed*
*4 egg yolks*
*¼ cup cream*
*1 teaspoon prepared mustard*
*salt and freshly ground black pepper*

Melt butter in a saucepan. Add lemon juice. Stir in peppercorns, egg yolks, cream, and mustard. Cook over gentle heat until sauce thickens. Do not allow sauce to boil. Season to taste with salt and pepper. *Makes ³⁄4 cup.*

## HOLLANDAISE SAUCE

*50 g butter*
*1 tablespoon lemon juice*
*2 egg yolks*
*¼ cup cream*
*½ teaspoon dry mustard*
*¼ teaspoon salt*

Melt the butter in a double boiler. Add lemon juice, egg yolks and cream. Cook, stirring constantly, until thick and smooth. Do not boil or sauce will curdle. Remove from heat. Add mustard and salt and beat until smooth. *Makes ³⁄4 cup.*

## PESTO

Pesto is a thick sauce that originated in Italy. Traditionally made with basil, parmesan cheese, pinenuts and olive oil, pesto is superb tossed through hot pasta or used as a tasty spread. The sauce can be frozen, but the texture will alter slightly.

*1 tablespoon oil*
*2 tablespoons pinenuts*
*3 cloves garlic, chopped*
*2 cups fresh basil leaves*
*¼ cup oil*
*salt and pepper to season*

Heat first measure of oil in a small frying pan. Add pinenuts and cook, stirring frequently, until golden. Drain on absorbent paper. Put the garlic, basil and pinenuts into the bowl of a food processor or blender. Process until finely chopped. Continue processing while adding second measure of oil in a thin, steady stream. Process for a few seconds until just combined. Season with salt and pepper to taste. *Makes about ½ cup.*

## SATAY SAUCE

2 tablespoons oil
1 clove garlic, crushed
1 onion, chopped
¼–½ teaspoon chilli powder
  (according to taste)
½ cup crunchy peanut butter
1 tablespoon soy sauce
1 tablespoon brown sugar
¾ cup coconut cream
salt and freshly ground black pepper

Heat oil in a saucepan. Add garlic, onion and chilli powder. Cook until onion is clear. Stir in peanut butter, soy sauce and sugar. Add coconut cream. Cook until mixture boils, stirring constantly. Season to taste with salt and pepper. *Makes 1¼ cups.*

## SPICY BARBECUE SAUCE

1 cup tomato sauce
½ cup water
3 tablespoons golden syrup
1 teaspoon salt
2 teaspoons Worcestershire sauce
½ teaspoon curry powder
freshly ground black pepper
1 clove garlic, crushed
¼ cup dry red wine

Combine all ingredients. Leave to stand for 5–6 hours. *Makes 2 cups.*

## TARTARE SAUCE

1 cup Mayonnaise (see page 181)
1 tablespoon chopped parsley
1 tablespoon finely chopped capers
  or gherkins
1 tablespoon finely chopped onion

Combine all ingredients. *Makes 1 cup.*

## WHITE SAUCE

2 tablespoons butter
2 tablespoons Champion standard
  grade flour
1 cup milk
salt and freshly ground black pepper

Melt butter in a small saucepan. Add flour and stir constantly for 2 minutes. Remove from heat. Gradually add milk, stirring constantly. Return pan to the heat, stirring continuously until sauce thickens and comes to the boil. Season to taste with salt and pepper. *Makes 1 cup.*

## BÉCHAMEL SAUCE

Stud an **onion** with **6 cloves**. Place onion in **1 cup milk** and bring almost to the boil. Strain. In a separate pan melt **2 tablespoons butter** and continue as for White Sauce above. Add heated milk.

## CHEESE SAUCE

After cooking White Sauce above, remove pan from heat. Stir in ½ **cup grated tasty cheddar cheese.**

## CURRY SAUCE

In the White Sauce recipe above, include **1–2 teaspoons curry powder** when adding flour.

## ONION SAUCE

Add **1 sliced onion** to butter in the White Sauce recipe and cook until soft. Continue as above.

## PARSLEY SAUCE

After cooking White Sauce above, remove pan from heat. Add **2–4 tablespoons chopped parsley.**

# WEIGHTS AND MEASURES

*New Zealand Standard metric cup and spoon measures are used in all recipes.*
*All measurements are level.*
*Easy measuring* — use measuring cups or jugs for liquid measures and sets of 1 cup, ½ cup, ⅓ cup and ¼ cup for dry ingredients.
*Brown sugar measurements* — are firmly packed so that the sugar will hold the shape of the cup when tipped out.
*Eggs* — No. 6 eggs are used as the standard size.

### ABBREVIATIONS

l = litre
ml = millilitre
cm = centimetre
mm = millimetre
g = gram
kg = kilogram
°C = degrees celsius

### STANDARD MEASURES

1 cup = 250 millilitres
1 litre = 4 cups
1 tablespoon = 15 millilitres
1 dessertspoon = 10 millilitres
1 teaspoon = 5 millilitres
½ teaspoon = 2.5 millilitres
¼ teaspoon = 1.25 millilitres

### APPROXIMATE METRIC/IMPERIAL CONVERSIONS IN COMMON COOKING USE

| WEIGHT | VOLUME | MEASUREMENTS |
| --- | --- | --- |
| 25 g = 1 ounce | 1 litre = 1¾ pints | 1 cm = ½ inch |
| 125 g = 4 ounces | | 20 cm = 8 inches |
| 225 g = 8 ounces | | 30 cm = 12 inches |
| 500 g = 1 pound | | |
| 1 kg = 2¼ pounds | | |

### WEIGHTS AND MEASURES — APPROXIMATE EQUIVALENTS

| ITEM | MEASURE | WEIGHT |
| --- | --- | --- |
| breadcrumbs (fresh) | 1 cup | 50 g |
| butter | 2 tablespoons | 30 g |
| cheese (grated, firmly packed) | 1 cup | 100 g |
| cocoa | 4 tablespoons | 25 g |
| coconut | 1 cup | 75 g |
| cornflour | 4 tablespoons | 25 g |
| cream | ½ pint | 300 ml |
| dried fruit (currants, sultanas, raisins, dates) | 1 cup | 150–175 g |
| flour | 1 cup | 125 g |
| golden syrup | 1 tablespoon | 25 g |
| milk | 1 cup | 250 ml |
| oil | 1 tablespoon | 15 ml |
| rice, sago | 2 tablespoons | 25 g |
| | 1 cup | 200 g |
| salt | 2 tablespoons | 25 g |
| sugar, white | 2 tablespoons | 30 g |
| | 1 cup | 250 g |
| sugar, brown | 1 cup (firmly packed) | 200 g |
| | 1 cup (loosely packed) | 125–150 g |
| sugar, icing | 1 cup | 150 g |
| standard No. 6 egg | | about 50 g |

# BEFORE AND AFTER EQUIVALENT MEASURES
## APPROXIMATE AMOUNTS NEEDED TO GIVE MEASURES:

⅓ cup uncooked rice = 1 cup cooked rice
⅓ cup uncooked pasta = 1 cup cooked pasta
2–3 chicken pieces = 1 cup cooked chicken
100 g cheese = 1 cup grated cheese
75 g mushrooms = 1 cup sliced = ½ cup cooked
4 toast slices bread = 1 cup fresh beadcrumbs
200 g (two) potatoes = 1 cup mashed potato

## OVEN CONVERSIONS
160°C = 325°F
180°C = 350°F
190°C = 375°F
200°C = 400°F

## A GUIDE TO OVEN TEMPERATURES AND USE

| PRODUCT | °C | °F | GAS NO. | DESCRIPTION |
|---|---|---|---|---|
| meringues, pavlova | 110–140 | 225–275 | ¼–1 | slow |
| custards, milk puddings, shortbread, rich fruit cakes, casseroles, slow roasting | 150–160 | 300–325 | 2–3 | moderately slow |
| biscuits, large and small cakes | 180–190 | 350–375 | 4–5 | moderate |
| roasting, sponges, muffins, short pastry | 190–220 | 375–425 | 5–6 | moderately hot |
| flaky pastry, scones, browning toppings | 220–230 | 425–450 | 6–8 | hot |
| puff pastry | 250–260 | 475–500 | 9–10 | very hot |

## OVEN HINTS

*Oven racks* — position before turning oven on.

*Oven positions:*
*Bottom of Oven* — use for slow cooking and low temperature cooking
*Middle of Oven* — for moderate temperature cooking
*Above Middle* — for quick cooking and high temperature cooking
*Fan-forced ovens* — refer to the manufacturer's directions as the models vary.
*Preheat oven to required temperature before food preparation.*
Cooking temperatures and times are a guide only as ovens may vary.

# GLOSSARY

*Al dente:* Used to describe cooked pasta that is firm to the bite.

*Arborio rice* is a short grain rice predominantly grown in Italy. It is used as the basis of Italian-style risotto dishes. As arborio rice cooks, the starch released from the granule thickens the sauce, giving a creamy consistency.

*Bain marie* is a water bath. The dish of food to be cooked is placed in a larger dish and surrounded with hot water to come half to three-quarters of the way up the food dish. This provides a gentle, more even heat for mixtures that are sensitive to direct heat.

*Bake blind:* To place a piece of baking paper in an unbaked pastry case, fill with dried beans or rice, and bake. This enables the pastry to bake with a flat base. Beans or rice for baking blind can be stored and re-used.

*Baking paper* has a special coating on it to prevent sticking. It saves greasing tins or baking trays. For cake or slice tins, line the base of the tin with baking paper. There is no need to grease the sides of the tin. Once the food is cooked, run a knife around the edges of the tin, pressing the knife blade against the tin to prevent damaging the cake or slice. Cover baking trays with baking paper to save greasing when baking biscuits.

*Baking powder* is a mixture of cream of tartar and baking soda plus wheat fillers, which helps the baking powder to flow easily.

*Baking soda* is also known as bicarbonate of soda.

*Basmati rice* is an aromatic long grain rice with a nutty flavour. Basmati rice is used extensively in Indian cuisine.

*Baste:* To spoon juices or marinades over foods being roasted to prevent drying and to give a glossy surface.

*Blanch:* To place fruit and vegetables in boiling water briefly, then remove to cold water to ease removing of skins or prepare for freezing.

*Blend:* To mix ingredients thoroughly to get an even consistency.

*Boil:* To cook at boiling point with large rolling bubbles forming.

*Bouquet garni* is a mixture of parsley, thyme and bay leaf which is tied together with cotton if fresh herbs are used, or enclosed in a muslin bag if dried herbs are used. Bouquet garni is used as a flavouring for stocks. It should be removed once the cooking is completed.

*Braise:* To gently fry in fat, then cook slowly in very little moisture, covered.

*Bulgar,* also known as *burghul,* is a type of cracked wheat with a distinctive nutty flavour. It is used extensively in Middle Eastern cuisine and is the basis of the salad tabouleh.

*Chicken:* To test whether chicken is cooked, pierce it in the thickest part with a skewer, satay stick or sharp knife. If the juices run clear, the chicken is cooked. If the juices are pink, further cooking is necessary.

*Chilli oil* is oil flavoured with fresh chillies. It can be bought already flavoured or fresh chillies can be steeped in oil to flavour your own. Use any oil you prefer, depending on its end use.

*Chocolate curls* are easily made using a potato peeler and 'peeling' a piece of chocolate. Well-formed curls will be made if the chocolate is slightly soft.

*Clarified butter* is butter from which milk solids have been removed. Can be used for frying as it heats to a high temperature without burning. Known also as frying butter or ghee.

*Coconut* throughout this cookbook means desiccated unless otherwise stated. Coconut can be toasted by heating it in a frying pan over a moderate heat. Shake the pan from time to time. Remove pan from heat when coconut just starts to colour.

*Coconut cream* or *coconut milk* is available canned or powdered, or can be made by mixing 1¼ cups of coconut with 300 ml of boiling water, then straining through a sieve and reserving the liquid. This will give about 1 cup (250 ml) of coconut milk.

*Cold-smoked salmon* has a translucent look and is smoked without heat.

*Cool pastry fillings:* Cold fillings should be used in pastry shells to prevent pastry becoming soggy on the bottom.

*Cornflour* is made from maize and is a starch used to thicken products such as sauces and desserts, or it can be used in some baked products.

*Couscous* is fluffy grains of semolina which are steamed and served like rice. Couscous is used extensively in Moroccan cooking.

*Cream:* To beat softened butter or other fat with sugar until light, fluffy and creamy in colour.

*Curry powder* is a mixture of spices and you can combine different spices in different amounts to make your own blend. Some of the basic spices might include cumin, coriander, ginger, cloves, fenugreek, turmeric and cinnamon. Whole spices can be ground with a mortar and pestle, or prepared ground spices can be used.

*Cut in:* Using a knife, pastry blender, food processor or clean fingertips to combine fat with flour to get a crumb-like consistency.

*Eggs* should be at room temperature when making sponges and other baked goods as this produces a cake with better volume. Egg whites for making meringues and pavlovas should always be at room temperature.

*Filo pastry* is tissue-paper-thin pastry traditionally used for strudels. It can be bought in packets from the chiller and once opened should be used within a week to 10 days. When working with filo pastry (sometimes written as phyllo) place it under a damp teatowel to prevent it from drying out and becoming brittle and hard to manage.

*Flour:* As a rule of thumb, use standard grade flour for baking and high grade flour for pastry, breads, doughs and heavy fruit cakes.

*Fold:* Combining a delicate mixture with a heavier one by using a metal spoon in a cutting action, cutting down through centre and bringing bottom mixture to top. Used for additions of whipped cream and beaten egg whites.

*Fresh and dried herbs:* As a rule of thumb, replace a measure of fresh herbs with half the quantity of dried herbs. Double a dried measure if replacing with fresh herbs.

*Fresh ginger* is root ginger. This is available from the fruit and vegetables section of the supermarket and should be stored in the refrigerator crisper or frozen for easy grating. The ginger root can be peeled before using if wished.

*Frothy:* When making white sauce, heat butter and flour until mixture appears frothy with small bubbles before adding liquid.

*Hot-smoked salmon* has the look of cooked fish and has been smoked with heat.

*Jelly bag:* A muslin or fine cloth bag that can be hung to allow jelly to drain through when preserving. A piece of muslin can be used for the same task. Attach this to the legs of an upturned chair before the jelly is drained through.

*Knead:* To press non-yeast doughs together to get an even texture. Yeast doughs are stretched and folded to develop elasticity. This is done by pushing the dough away from you with the heel of your hand, then folding the dough over.

*Lemons:* Two main lemon types are grown in New Zealand, Meyer and Lisbon. Meyer lemons have a soft bright yellow flesh and semi-sweet flavour. They make a good garnish but do not have a lot of flavour in cooking. Lisbon lemons have a light, hard skin, a light lemon flesh and a sharper lemon taste. They should always be used in cooking where setting is required, as in condensed-milk cheesecakes, lemon honey and lemon meringue pies.

*Margarine* can replace butter, giving a similar result. Extra flour may need to be added in some baked recipes to give the required consistency.

*Marinate:* To leave meat, poultry or fish in a tenderising or flavouring liquid (the marinade) for a period of time.

*Mash:* Food is crushed until soft. This can be done with a fork or a potato masher.

*Measuring:* All recipes in this book have been developed using standard metric measuring cups and spoons. All measurements are level. For easiest measuring use measuring cups or jugs for liquid measures and sets of 1 cup, ½ cup and ¼ cup for dry ingredients. Brown sugar measures are firmly packed so that the sugar will hold the shape of the cup when tipped out.

*Nuts* can be toasted in the oven or in a pan on top of the stove. To toast nuts in the oven, place in an oven dish and cook at 180°C for 5–15 minutes, depending on the nuts. To toast on top of the stove, place nuts in a frying pan and cook over a moderate heat until just starting to colour. Toss nuts during cooking to prevent burning.

*Olive oil* is available in a variety of types. Light olive oil has the least flavour, with the deeper green virgin olive oils having a distinct flavour. Use olive oil to make French dressing or vinaigrette. If using olive oil in cooking, take care not to overheat it as it will smoke at a lower temperature than many oils.

*Polenta* is a ground corn (cornmeal), which is a staple food of northern Italy. It is boiled in water, producing a thick porridge-like mixture, which is then left to solidify.

*Prepared mustard* is wet mustard that has already been made or bought. Wholeseed (wholegrain) or smooth varieties are available.

*Purée:* Cooked fruit or vegetables mashed or sieved to give a smooth semi-liquid product.

*Roasted capsicums:* Cut capsicums in half lengthwise. Remove core and place cut-side down on a baking tray. Bake at 200°C for 15 minutes or until skins are blistered and browned. When capsicums are cool enough to handle, remove skin. The skins on red and yellow capsicums will blister and come away more easily than green capsicums.

*Rub in:* To mix fat into flour by rubbing with fingers to get a crumb-like mixture.

*Sambal oelek* is a paste made from hot chillies and salt.

*Sauté:* To fry food in a small amount of hot fat quickly and with shaking or stirring of pan to get even cooking.

*Scald:* Liquids are brought to boiling point.

*Setting test for jam or jelly:* Put a little jam or jelly on a cold plate. Leave to cool slightly. The mixture will set if the surface wrinkles when touched, and a channel formed (when a finger is drawn through) remains open.

*Shallots* are small brown-skinned onions similar in shape to a chestnut or large, slightly flat garlic clove. They have a mild onion flavour and are good for use in salads, dressings and casseroles or anything that requires a milder onion flavour.

*Shards* are long pointed pieces that look like broken glass. Praline is often broken into shards for impressive decoration.

*Sieve:* To pass through a mesh to get an even consistency.

*Sift:* To pass dry ingredients through a mesh to remove lumps and/or foreign matter, or to mix evenly.

*Simmer:* To cook just at boiling point, not a full rolling boil.

*Skim:* To remove fat or scum from the surface of a liquid with a slotted spoon, spoon or absorbent paper.

*Soft breadcrumbs* are made from stale bread. They are not toasted.

*Softened butter* makes creaming butter and sugar easy. Butter can be softened in the microwave, left to stand in a warm place or softened over hot water. Softened butter is not the same as melted butter.

*Spoons:* A wooden spoon is used for stirring a heated mixture, as it does not become too hot to handle. It does not discolour pale mixtures as a metal one can do by scraping against the metal of the saucepan. Metal spoons, solid or slotted, are used for transferring foods; slotted ones will allow liquids to drain from solids. Slotted spoons are useful for folding mixtures together. A metal spoon is best for folding or creaming butter and sugar by hand.

*Steep:* To leave food or flavouring to stand in liquid to absorb flavours.

*Stiffly beaten egg white:* Beaten until peaks formed will hold their shape, but tips bend over. Mixture should be glossy.

*Stir-fry:* To stir and toss prepared ingredients in hot oil very quickly, resulting in moist meats and crisp vegetables.

*Stock* can be homemade or bought in cartons as a liquid, in pots as a powder or as foil-wrapped cubes. One stock cube is the equivalent of 1 teaspoon of stock powder.

*Tahini* is a paste made from toasted sesame seeds and is widely used in Middle Eastern cooking. It has a toasted-nut flavour.

*Tepid:* This is blood temperature, i.e. 37°C, and liquid feels neither hot nor cold when a drop is placed on the back of your hand.

*Thick and glossy:* When making meringue, egg whites and sugar are beaten until very stiff. This is when peaks stand up after the beaters are removed. The meringue should look shiny. An electric mixer should be used for this as it takes time and is too arduous to do by hand successfully. The sugar should be dissolved in the egg whites. Test by rubbing a little mixture between your fingers.

*To cover steamed puddings:* Tear a sheet of foil about 5 cm larger than the top of the basin. Make a pleat right across the sheet of foil. Cover basin with foil. Tie string very tightly around pudding basin just under the lip. Take a separate piece of string about 40 cm in length and fold in half. Secure the string at opposite ends of the basin to make a handle. This helps to get the pudding basin in and out of the saucepan.

*Tomato paste* is concentrated tomato purée.

*Tomato purée* is available in cans or can be made from fresh tomatoes in a blender or food processor.

*Unmoulding jellies:* A vacuum forms in the bottom of a jelly mould and this needs to be broken to release the jelly. Dip the mould in a bowl of hot water three times. Press the jelly around the edge, pulling it away gently with your finger. Turn mould onto a plate and shake sharply as you hold the plate and mould.

*Yeast* is used to raise bread, etc. 1 tablespoon of Edmonds active yeast (dried granules) equals 2 tablespoons of Edmonds Surebake active yeast mixture.

# INDEX

## CAKES

Almond Crumble Cake . . . . . . . . . . . . . . . . 11
Apple Sultana Cake . . . . . . . . . . . . . . . . . . . 11
Chocolate Chip Speckle Cake . . . . . . . . . . 12
Cinnamon Pecan Cake . . . . . . . . . . . . . . . . 13
Coconut Cake . . . . . . . . . . . . . . . . . . . . . . . 14
Coffee Cake . . . . . . . . . . . . . . . . . . . . . . . . 14
Date Cake . . . . . . . . . . . . . . . . . . . . . . . . . 17
Ginger Ale Fruit Cake . . . . . . . . . . . . . . . . 17
Ginger Cake . . . . . . . . . . . . . . . . . . . . . . . . 17
Lemon Curd and Yoghurt Cake . . . . . . . . . . 18
Moist Apple Walnut Cake . . . . . . . . . . . . . . 18
Moist Chocolate Cake . . . . . . . . . . . . . . . . . 20
Orange Polenta Cake . . . . . . . . . . . . . . . . . 20
Plum Cake . . . . . . . . . . . . . . . . . . . . . . . . . 22
Rhubarb and Pecan Crust Cake . . . . . . . . . . 22
Spiced Feijoa Cake . . . . . . . . . . . . . . . . . . . 23

## BISCUITS

Almond Crescent Biscuits . . . . . . . . . . . . . . 25
Almond Shortbread Rings . . . . . . . . . . . . . . 25
Chocolate Brownie Biscuits . . . . . . . . . . . . . 26
Coffee Kisses . . . . . . . . . . . . . . . . . . . . . . . 26
Espresso Biscuits with Fudge Filling . . . . . . . 27
Ginger Biscuits . . . . . . . . . . . . . . . . . . . . . . 27
Hazelnut Shortbread Fingers . . . . . . . . . . . . 28
Macadamia Nut and
    White Chocolate Biscuits . . . . . . . . . . . . . 28
Orange Melting Moments . . . . . . . . . . . . . . 29
Yoghurt Raisin Biscuits . . . . . . . . . . . . . . . . 29

## SLICES

Apple Shortcake Squares . . . . . . . . . . . . . . . 31
Apricot and Pistachio Nut Slice . . . . . . . . . . 31
Caramel Date Fingers . . . . . . . . . . . . . . . . . 33
Coconut and Almond Slice . . . . . . . . . . . . . 34
Coconut Chocolate Brownies . . . . . . . . . . . . 33
Coffee Oat Slice . . . . . . . . . . . . . . . . . . . . . 34
Coffee Walnut Slice . . . . . . . . . . . . . . . . . . 35
Honey Nut Bars . . . . . . . . . . . . . . . . . . . . . 35
Nutty Crunch Slice . . . . . . . . . . . . . . . . . . . 36
Oaty Date Bars . . . . . . . . . . . . . . . . . . . . . . 37
Rocky Road Slice . . . . . . . . . . . . . . . . . . . . 38
White and Dark Chocolate Brownie Slice . . . . 38

## MUFFINS, LOAVES AND TARTLETS

Feta and Parsley Muffins . . . . . . . . . . . . . . . 41
Fresh Lemon Loaf . . . . . . . . . . . . . . . . . . . . 42
Fruit Tartlets . . . . . . . . . . . . . . . . . . . . . . . 44
Gingerbread Loaf . . . . . . . . . . . . . . . . . . . . 42
Mini Pecan Tartlets . . . . . . . . . . . . . . . . . . 45
Tiny Cheese Muffins . . . . . . . . . . . . . . . . . . 41
Tiny Lemon Curd Tartlets . . . . . . . . . . . . . . 45

## FINGER FOODS

Antipasto . . . . . . . . . . . . . . . . . . . . . . . . . . 49
Blue Cheese Spread . . . . . . . . . . . . . . . . . . 49
Cheese Ball . . . . . . . . . . . . . . . . . . . . . . . . 49

Devilled Almonds . . . . . . . . . . . . . . . . . . . . 49
Felafel with Yoghurt Sauce . . . . . . . . . . . . . 50
Guacamole . . . . . . . . . . . . . . . . . . . . . . . . . 52
Mixed Satays with Peanut Dip . . . . . . . . . . . 50
Parmesan and Garlic Twists . . . . . . . . . . . . . 52
Prosciutto-wrapped Asparagus . . . . . . . . . . . 53
Quick Peanut Dip . . . . . . . . . . . . . . . . . . . . 54
Sesame Chicken Sticks . . . . . . . . . . . . . . . . 55
Sesame-marinated Chicken Nibbles . . . . . . . . 55
Spicy Cajun Potato Wedges . . . . . . . . . . . . . 57
Spring Rolls with Chilli Dipping Sauce . . . . . . 57
Sushi . . . . . . . . . . . . . . . . . . . . . . . . . . . . . 58

## LIGHT MEALS

Chicken Enchiladas . . . . . . . . . . . . . . . . . . . 63
Crispy-skinned Potatoes with
    Bacon and Avocado Filling . . . . . . . . . . . . 63
Curried Vegetable Parcels . . . . . . . . . . . . . . 64
Feta, Olive and Sundried Tomato Calzone . . . 65
Ham and Vegetable Frittata . . . . . . . . . . . . . 66
Kumara Soup . . . . . . . . . . . . . . . . . . . . . . . 67
Lamb Satay . . . . . . . . . . . . . . . . . . . . . . . . 69
Leek and Potato Soup . . . . . . . . . . . . . . . . . 69
Marinated Pork Spare Ribs . . . . . . . . . . . . . 69
Mexican Quesadillas . . . . . . . . . . . . . . . . . . 70
Mini Meat Pies . . . . . . . . . . . . . . . . . . . . . 70
Onion Marmalade . . . . . . . . . . . . . . . . . . . . 74
Potato, Cauliflower and Chickpea Curry . . . . 71
Pumpkin and Chicken Filo Pies . . . . . . . . . . 72
Spinach and Feta Filo Parcels . . . . . . . . . . . 72
Summer Calzone . . . . . . . . . . . . . . . . . . . . 73
Super Sandwiches . . . . . . . . . . . . . . . . . . . . 74
Tabouleh . . . . . . . . . . . . . . . . . . . . . . . . . . 74
Tostadas . . . . . . . . . . . . . . . . . . . . . . . . . . 77
Turkish Lamb Patties with
    Yoghurt Sauce and Pita Bread . . . . . . . . . . 77

## SALADS

Chicken and Asparagus Salad
    with Mustard Dressing . . . . . . . . . . . . . . . 79
Grilled Chicken Caesar Salad . . . . . . . . . . . . 79
Lunchbox Pasta Salad . . . . . . . . . . . . . . . . . 80
Orzo Pasta Salad . . . . . . . . . . . . . . . . . . . . 80
Salmon and Pasta Niçoise Salad . . . . . . . . . . 81
Smoked Chicken, Pawpaw and
    Macadamia Nut Salad . . . . . . . . . . . . . . . 83
Spinach, Feta and Bacon Salad . . . . . . . . . . . 83
Thai-style Beef Salad . . . . . . . . . . . . . . . . . 84
Tuna Pasta Salad . . . . . . . . . . . . . . . . . . . . 84
Warm Mediterranean Lamb Salad . . . . . . . . 86
Wild Rice Salad . . . . . . . . . . . . . . . . . . . . . 87

## MAIN MEALS

Beef, Cashew Nut and Vegetable Stir-fry
    in Black Bean Sauce . . . . . . . . . . . . . . . . 91
Beef Fajitas . . . . . . . . . . . . . . . . . . . . . . . . 91
Chargrilled Vegetable Lasagne . . . . . . . . . . . 92
Cheesy Sesame-coated Chicken . . . . . . . . . . 93

Chicken and Avocado Risotto . . . . . . . . . . . 95
Chicken Cannelloni . . . . . . . . . . . . . . . . . .93
Chicken Chow Mein . . . . . . . . . . . . . . 95
Chicken Curry . . . . . . . . . . . . . . . . . 95
Chilli Con Carne . . . . . . . . . . . . . . . . 96
Deep-pan Pizza . . . . . . . . . . . . . . . 108
Grilled Fish with Parmesan Crust . . . . . . . . 96
Hamburgers . . . . . . . . . . . . . . . . . . . 97
Lamb and Prune Tagine . . . . . . . . . . . . 99
Lamb and Vegetable Stir-fry . . . . . . . . . . . 99
Lamb Curry . . . . . . . . . . . . . . . . . 100
Lanterna Pasta with Roasted
    Vegetables and Pesto . . . . . . . . . . . 100
Moroccan Lamb and Couscous Pilaf . . . . . . 101
Moussaka . . . . . . . . . . . . . . . . . . . . 102
Mushroom Risotto . . . . . . . . . . . . . . . . 103
Mussels in Tomato Sauce . . . . . . . . . . . . . 103
Pasta with Pesto, Crispy Bacon
    and Walnuts . . . . . . . . . . . . . . . . . . 104
Penne Pasta with Broccoli and
    Blue Cheese Sauce . . . . . . . . . . . . . . 105
Pesto and Blue Cheese Rigati . . . . . . . . . . 105
Pizza Dough . . . . . . . . . . . . . . . . . . . 107
Pork and Noodle Stir-fry . . . . . . . . . . . . . 109
Pork and Spinach Risotto . . . . . . . . . . . . 110
Pumpkin and Leek Risotto . . . . . . . . . . . . 111
Quick Thai Green Chicken Curry . . . . . . . 113
Ricciolini Pasta with Pumpkin,
    Feta and Basil . . . . . . . . . . . . . . . . . 113
Salmon Rissoles . . . . . . . . . . . . . . . . . 114
Seafood Risotto . . . . . . . . . . . . . . . . . 114
Spiced Chicken Pilaf . . . . . . . . . . . . . 115
Stuffed Baked Capsicums . . . . . . . . . . . . 116
Sundried Tomato and Feta-stuffed
    Chicken Breasts . . . . . . . . . . . . . . . 117
Tandoori Chicken Breasts . . . . . . . . . . . 119
Thai-style Beef and Baby Corn Stir-fry . . . . . 119
Tomato Sauce . . . . . . . . . . . . . . . . . 107
Topping Combinations for Pizza . . . . . . . . .107
Torroncini Napolitana . . . . . . . . . . . . . . 119

DESSERTS
Baked Lemon Cheesecake . . . . . . . . . . . . 123
Banana Pancakes . . . . . . . . . . . . . . . . . 123
Cheese Categories . . . . . . . . . . . . . . . . 124
Cheeseboards . . . . . . . . . . . . . . . . . . . 124
Chocolate and Almond Stuffed Peaches . . . . 127
Chocolate Dessert Cake . . . . . . . . . . . . . 127
Chocolate-garnished Hazelnut
    Meringue Torte . . . . . . . . . . . . . . . 128
Coffee Liqueur Cheesecake . . . . . . . . . . . 129
Fresh Summer Fruit Platter with
    Raspberry Crème Fraîche Dip . . . . . . . . 129
Ice-cream . . . . . . . . . . . . . . . . . . . . 131
Ice-cream Terrine —
    Chocolate and Apricot . . . . . . . . . . . . 131
Individual Pineapple and Ginger
    Steamed Puddings . . . . . . . . . . . . . 133
Passionfruit Flan . . . . . . . . . . . . . . . . . 133
Pavlova Roll with Apricot Filling . . . . . . . . 134
Pear, Apple and Ginger Crumble
    with Custard . . . . . . . . . . . . . . . . . 134

Spiced Pumpkin Pie . . . . . . . . . . . . . . . 136
Upside-down Pudding . . . . . . . . . . . . . . 136
Warm Gingerbread Date Cake . . . . . . . . . 137
Zuccotto . . . . . . . . . . . . . . . . . . . . . 137

CHRISTMAS
Christmas Cookies . . . . . . . . . . . . . . 144
Hazelnut Chocolate Truffles . . . . . . . . . . . 144
Lemon Star Biscuits . . . . . . . . . . . . . . 145
Panettone . . . . . . . . . . . . . . . . . . . . 146
Panforte . . . . . . . . . . . . . . . . . . . . .145
Stained-glass-window Log . . . . . . . . . . . . 147
Tiramisù Terrine . . . . . . . . . . . . . . . . 147

CHRISTMAS DINNER MENU 1
Roast Chicken with Wild Rice
    and Cashew Nut Stuffing . . . . . . . . . . 141
Vegetables . . . . . . . . . . . . . . . . . . . . 141

CHRISTMAS DINNER MENU 2
Aioli . . . . . . . . . . . . . . . . . . . . . . . 143
Hot Orange-glazed Ham on the Bone . . . . . 142
Medley of Summer Vegetables . . . . . . . . . 143
Minted Baby Potatoes . . . . . . . . . . . . . . 143
Pawpaw and Coriander Salsa . . . . . . . . . . 142

EASTER
Apricot-stuffed Forequarter . . . . . . . . . . . 149
Easter Biscuits . . . . . . . . . . . . . . . . . . 149

TRADITIONAL FARE
Beef Casserole . . . . . . . . . . . . . . . . . 152
Beef Wellington . . . . . . . . . . . . . . . . . 153
Boned Pork Loin with
    Spinach and Prune Stuffing . . . . . . . . . 154
Braised Lamb Knuckles
    in a Rich Gravy . . . . . . . . . . . . . . . . 154
Chocolate Chip Biscuits . . . . . . . . . . . . . 161
Individual Pavlovas . . . . . . . . . . . . . . . 159
Old-fashioned Vegetable Soup . . . . . . . . . 151
Pea and Ham Soup . . . . . . . . . . . . . . . 151
Peppered Eye-fillet Steaks
    with Béarnaise Sauce . . . . . . . . . . . . 156
Quick Apple and Berry Crumble . . . . . . . . 159
Rack of Lamb with a Rosemary Crust . . . . . 157
Rice Pudding . . . . . . . . . . . . . . . . . . . 159
Spinach and Cheese Soufflé . . . . . . . . . . . 151
Sponge Roll . . . . . . . . . . . . . . . . . . . 160
Steamed Chocolate Puddings . . . . . . . . . . 160

BARBECUE MENU
Bacon-wrapped Sausages . . . . . . . . . . . . 163
Barbecued Vegetables . . . . . . . . . . . . . . 163
Garlic and Sweet Chilli Prawns . . . . . . . . . 163
Honey and Thyme
    Marinated Chicken Breasts . . . . . . . . . . 163

PRESERVES
Apple and Passionfruit Jelly . . . . . . . . . . . 167
Apricot Curd . . . . . . . . . . . . . . . . . . . 167
Chargrilled Capsicums with
    Garlic and Rosemary . . . . . . . . . . . . 172

Dried Fruit Compote . . . . . . . . . . . . . . . . . 169
Honey and Beer Mustard . . . . . . . . . . . . . 173
Marinated Olives with Herbs . . . . . . . . . . 174
Olive Tapenade . . . . . . . . . . . . . . . . . . . . 177
Oven-dried Tomatoes . . . . . . . . . . . . . . . 175
Peach Conserve . . . . . . . . . . . . . . . . . . . . 170
Peaches in Spiced Brandy . . . . . . . . . . . . . 170
Refrigerated Fig and Orange Jam . . . . . . . . 167
Refrigerated Orange, Lime
   and Ginger Marmalade . . . . . . . . . . . . . 168
Roasted Red Capsicum
   and Coriander Pesto . . . . . . . . . . . . . . . 177
Sundried Tomato Pesto . . . . . . . . . . . . . . 177
Walnut Pesto . . . . . . . . . . . . . . . . . . . . . 177
White Wine and Rosemary Mustard . . . . . . 173

ICINGS
Butter Icing . . . . . . . . . . . . . . . . . . . . . . 179
Chocolate Butter Icing . . . . . . . . . . . . . . 179
Chocolate Icing . . . . . . . . . . . . . . . . . . . 179
Coffee Icing . . . . . . . . . . . . . . . . . . . . . . 179
Cream Cheese Icing . . . . . . . . . . . . . . . . . 179
Lemon Icing . . . . . . . . . . . . . . . . . . . . . . 179
Melted Chocolate Icing (Ganache) . . . . . . . 179
Orange Icing . . . . . . . . . . . . . . . . . . . . . . 179
White Icing . . . . . . . . . . . . . . . . . . . . . . 179

Lemon Curd . . . . . . . . . . . . . . . . . . . . . . .179

PASTRIES
Flaky Pastry . . . . . . . . . . . . . . . . . . . . . . 179
Food-processor Short Pastry . . . . . . . . . . . 180
Nut Pastry . . . . . . . . . . . . . . . . . . . . . . . 180
Puff Pastry . . . . . . . . . . . . . . . . . . . . . . . 180

Short Pastry . . . . . . . . . . . . . . . . . . . . . . 180
Spice Pastry . . . . . . . . . . . . . . . . . . . . . . 180
Sweet Shortcrust Pastry . . . . . . . . . . . . . . 180
Wholemeal Pastry . . . . . . . . . . . . . . . . . . 180

DRESSINGS
Avocado Dressing . . . . . . . . . . . . . . . . . . 180
Blue Cheese Dressing . . . . . . . . . . . . . . . . 180
Caesar Salad Dressing . . . . . . . . . . . . . . . 181
French Dressing (Vinaigrette) . . . . . . . . . . 181
Mayonnaise . . . . . . . . . . . . . . . . . . . . . . 181
Mustard Dressing . . . . . . . . . . . . . . . . . . 181
Quick Blender Mayonnaise . . . . . . . . . . . . 181
Uncooked (Condensed Milk)
   Salad Dressing . . . . . . . . . . . . . . . . . . . 181
Yoghurt Dressing . . . . . . . . . . . . . . . . . . 181

SAUCES
Apple Sauce . . . . . . . . . . . . . . . . . . . . . . 181
Béarnaise Sauce . . . . . . . . . . . . . . . . . . . 182
Béchamel Sauce . . . . . . . . . . . . . . . . . . . 183
Cheese Sauce . . . . . . . . . . . . . . . . . . . . . 183
Cucumber and Mint Raita . . . . . . . . . . . . 182
Curry Sauce . . . . . . . . . . . . . . . . . . . . . . 183
Green Peppercorn Sauce . . . . . . . . . . . . . 182
Hollandaise Sauce . . . . . . . . . . . . . . . . . . 182
Onion Sauce . . . . . . . . . . . . . . . . . . . . . 183
Parsley Sauce . . . . . . . . . . . . . . . . . . . . . 183
Pesto . . . . . . . . . . . . . . . . . . . . . . . . . . 182
Satay Sauce . . . . . . . . . . . . . . . . . . . . . . 183
Spicy Barbecue Sauce . . . . . . . . . . . . . . . 183
Tartare Sauce . . . . . . . . . . . . . . . . . . . . . 183
White Sauce . . . . . . . . . . . . . . . . . . . . . . 183

# ACKNOWLEDGEMENTS

*Tableware kindly supplied by:*
The Studio of Tableware, Mt Eden, Auckland
Milly's, Ponsonby, Auckland
Nest, Newmarket, Auckland
The Garden Party, Ponsonby, Auckland

ISBN 1-86958-844-4

© 2000 Text and Photography Bluebird Foods Ltd

First published in 2000 by Hodder Moa Beckett Publishers Ltd
[a member of the Hodder Headline Group],
4 Whetu Place, Mairangi Bay, Auckland, New Zealand

Art directed, designed, produced and typeset by Hodder Moa Beckett Publishers Ltd

Text and food styling by Sue Lyons
Photographs by Bruce Benson
Scanning and colour separations by Microdot, Auckland
Printed by Toppan Printing Co. Ltd, Hong Kong